The Reason
for Our Hope

The Reason
for Our Hope

by
VERNON C. GROUNDS
President, Conservative Baptist
Theological Seminary
Denver, Colorado

35c, 3 for $1.00

order from

BACK TO THE BIBLE PUBLISHERS

Box 233   Lincoln 1, Nebraska

(Published through special arrangement with Moody Press)

With gratitude and affection I dedicate
this book to all the members of the
congregation of the Gospel Tabernacle
who by their loyalty, intercession, and
co-operation contributed largely to whatever measure of blessing my ministry
among them may have enjoyed.

VERNON GROUNDS

Acknowledgments

I wish to express my thanks to the publishers who have kindly permitted me to quote from copyrighted books: Harper & Brothers, for quotations from *Anno Domini,* by Kenneth Scott Latourette, and *Man the Unknown,* by Alexis Carrel. The Judson Press, for quotations from *Bush Aglow,* by Richard Ellsworth Day. The Macmillan Company, for quotations from *The Modern Use of the Bible,* by Harry Emerson Fosdick, and *The Case for Christianity*, by C. S. Lewis. Acknowledgment is also made for use of the article, *Battle by the Bible,* reprinted by special permission of John Hix, creator of the newspaper feature "Strange As It Seems."

Sanctify the Lord God in your hearts: and be ready always to give an answer to every man that asketh you a reason of the hope that is in you with meekness and fear. —I Peter 3:15

Contents

Introduction

ALLAN A. MACRAE, Ph.D.

President, Faith Theological Seminary

It has been said that if an idea is repeated often enough, people will come to think that it is true. Certainly in recent years the idea has been reiterated over and over that Christianity is out of date and that men of education and learning no longer believe in the teachings of the Bible. Scoffers ridicule the statements of the Book which was the foundation of our American civilization, and many people assume that education and simple faith in the Scripture as God's Word do not go together.

In view of this situation, it is refreshing indeed to see the present volume of radio messages by Mr. Grounds. In clear and moving language he points out that the great truths of the Bible are just as true today as they ever were, and that no advance made by modern knowledge or modern research has done anything to shake them. As one reads his statements, one cannot but be amazed at the breadth of his reading. He has covered a wide section of contemporary opinion and draws on many sources to show the dependability of the Bible and its teachings.

Best of all, these sermons center around the divine Christ of Calvary, and place their emphasis upon His atonement as the answer to all human needs. The book deserves a wide reading. It can be read and reread profitably. May God use it to turn men's eyes to His Word and to His Son! May it lead many to increased study of the Bible and to renewed meditation upon its statements, in order that God's Word may shed its beams into the inner recesses of their hearts and may exert more widely that influence that is so much needed today.

There is a tendency in much preaching to neglect the essentials of the Christian faith and to deal with all sorts of matters which are outside the proper sphere of the Christian preacher. In the emphasis which Mr. Grounds places upon the Word of God, the Deity of Christ, and His atonement, he sets an example which must be followed by ministers today if the Church is to regain the place of influence in American society which it formerly held. The book should fill a great present need. May it stimulate many others to preach along similar lines and to emulate its gifted author in searching the Scriptures and in examining the evidences that support the divine claims of the Bible!

Christianity and Its Critics

> God so loved the world, that he gave his only begotten Son, that whosoever believeth in him should not perish, but have everlasting life.

MARTIN LUTHER said of John 3:16 that it is the Bible in miniature. For the very center and marrow of the Christian message is God's love for a lost and unloving world. Perhaps what strikes you most forcefully is the sheer incredibility of it. God created the world? Yes! God governs the world? Yes! God keeps the world going? Yes! But God loves the world? No!

Out of all the millions of the inhabitants of the earth, only a handful of human beings are stupid enough to swallow the nonsense of atheism; and one must be stupid indeed to subscribe to its dogmas. Reason and common sense cry out with united voice, "There is a God!" So overwhelming is the evidence for a Supreme Intelligence, a Sovereign Creator, that the Bible never stops to argue His existence. It simply assumes that God *is* and dismisses the skeptic with the stinging rebuke, "The fool hath said in his heart, There is no God."

Lieut. Col. Warren J. Clear relates how, while on Bataan, he and a tough sergeant took refuge together in a foxhole during a fierce Japanese attack. As the bullets sang out about them, both prayed aloud. When they emerged, Clear said to the sergeant, "You were praying, weren't you?" "Yes, sir," came the answer, "I was. There are no atheists in foxholes."

"The fool hath said in his heart, There is no God."

If you want any additional corroboration of man's instinctive faith in God when in the thick of danger and in the face of death, read that truly thrilling story by Lieut. James C. Whittaker, *We Thought We Heard the Angels Sing*. And what is his confession? "For me, our terrible twenty-one days on the Pacific represent the greatest adventure a man can have—finding his God. Before that adventure, I was an agnostic, an atheist, in other words. But there can be no atheist on rubber rafts any more than in the foxholes of Bataan."

One reason for a person's difficulty in believing the love of God is the unimaginable immensity of the universe when you compare it with the littleness of our earth. Many a serious skeptic cannot bring himself to believe that the God who presides over the immeasurable vastness of space should pay any particular attention to this comparatively microscopic planet on which we happen to find ourselves. Why should God care for this little speck of dust any more than a carpenter might care especially for some one nail which he had driven into a huge building?

To be sure, there is no point to denying that our earth is tiny when you consider it against the background of the whole universe. A few facts will illustrate this convincingly, I think. How much bigger than our earth do you suppose the sun is? Its diameter is 110 times larger than that of our planet, and its volume is 1,300,000 times as great. And yet, compared with other heavenly bodies, the sun is a tiny dot, a grain of sand. Take the star Betelgeuse which the astronomers have measured. Its diameter is about 240 million miles. That figure may be more meaningful when I say that we could pack into Betelgeuse about 25 million suns as large as the one which shines above us day after day. And you must remember that our whole solar system is but one of countless solar systems scattered across space.

In view of all this, one severe critic of Christianity, Dr. Harry Elmer Barnes, has said that before we knew facts such as these it "seemed reasonable that God should send His only begotten Son to serve as a vicarious sacrifice . . . but that the cosmic God, if there be one, has ever taken special cognizance of Jesus Christ . . . an insignificant religious teacher, who lived in ancient Palestine some two thousand years ago, represents a conception which can be entertained only by a person severely circumscribed by ignorance or limited in intellectual power. That this same religious teacher could have been, in any literal way, the only begotten Son of the Administrator of the cosmos is nonsense too childish to receive even passing comment."

But is it? Do the findings of modern astronomy make absurd those words which have always been considered sublime, "God so loved the world that he gave his only begotten Son"? Actually the findings of modern astronomy do nothing of the sort; everybody who argues in that fashion is guilty of a strange blunder. He is confusing mere bigness with value. What he is really contending is this: If a thing is big, it is therefore valuable; and if a thing is not big, it is by necessity of little value. Yet how stupid that is! A ton of coal has much greater bulk than a diamond of 5 karats; but if you had your choice, which would you take? Size, you see, has nothing to do with the worth of a thing. Let me illustrate in another way the stupidity of confusing mere bulk with value. In the home of a millionaire, there may be scores of rooms crowned with priceless articles collected from foreign countries; and, at the same time, in that home there may be an insignificant bundle of flesh and blood weighing only a few pounds, the millionaire's baby boy. A fire breaks out, and the flames begin to turn that home and all its treasures into smoke and ashes. Does the millionaire worry most about his pictures and furniture? Of course not! All he thinks about is his baby, and he would gladly have a dozen homes burn to the ground rather than have his baby hurt. That baby's small size is no criterion of his value. In the eyes of his father, he is worth more than a hundred homes which occupy thousands upon thousands of times more space than he does.

So it is with man and God. What are all the vast stretches of empty space to God? Are they valuable just because they are so big? Certainly not! One man with his capacity to love God, serve Him, worship and fellowship with Him is worth more than all the hugeness of empty space and senseless stars. Thus the Lord Jesus reduced things to their proper proportion when He said, "What shall it profit a man if he gain the whole world and lose his own soul?"

There is another reason, however, why a large number of honest and sober-minded folk find the message of John 3:16 incredible; and this reason, I think, is the most telling argument which its critics can level against Christianity.

The critics want to know how you can possibly believe that God loves the world when you consider all the pain and suffering and misery abounding on every side. Can this world with its multiplied woes be the creation of a loving God? The brutal facts fling a challenge into the teeth of Christianity, do they not?

When once a man starts to examine our whole human situation, he comes upon facts which compel him to ask, whether he wants to or not, "Is the King of the universe really our Friend?" God loves the world. But in India each year 3,000 people are torn to pieces by wild beasts, 20,000 are poisoned by the bites of terrible reptiles and 1,500,000 are killed by disease-carrying insects. God loves the world. But in Central China, annually, 40 out of every 100 children born perish with cold or famine before they are a year old. God loves the world. But in 1908 and again in 1920 earthquakes in Sicily and China swallowed a half-million people in sixty seconds. God loves the world. But in Russia, during a few years of revolution, Lenin massacred 1,750,000 of his countrymen and allowed probably 18,000,000 to die of famine. God loves the world. But in the Soviet Republic, according to a report in *Life,* over 10,000,000 people died a violent death in 1942. God loves the world. But in World War II intelligent human beings, herded together in the gigantic armies, were bent upon destroying one another with the wonderful machinery which their intelligence had devised. God loves the world. In the face of all this, in the face of life's pain and misery and, at times its stark insanity, can we believe that?

Yes, we can, provided we hold fast to one fact: *man's responsibility.* Who is to be blamed for the suffering which makes this world a vale of tears? Is it God's fault or man's? If it is God's, then surely He does not love us. It if is man's, however, then we can still believe the message of John 3:16. Whose fault is it then—God's or man's?

It is man's! For man is a free being, made in the image of God, and therefore able to choose how he will live and what he will do. He is not a machine—he is a man; and being man he has freedom to make real choices. Man is not a puppet—he is a person; and possession of personality implies freedom to make real choices. You see, in creating man, God was seeking a creature who could really serve Him, really obey Him, really love Him. Hence God made man a free person, not a piece of machinery; for only a free being can serve, obey, and love.

Man could be a real man only if free, able to serve God or able to defy Him, able to obey God or able to rebel against Him, able to love Him or able to hate Him. And all the evil in the world can be traced back ultimately to man's unforced, sinful choice. Instead of freely serving God, he elected to defy Him. Instead of freely obeying God, he elected to hate Him. And the result has been tragic. So God is not to be blamed for the suffering and misery abounding on every side. On the contrary, God in His love and grace is bending all His divine power to undo what man has done. And in His wisdom God is making the wrath of man to work out for human good and divine glory. The presence of all the pain in the world does not indicate that John 3:16 is incredible. It indicates, rather, that man is a rebel against God and because a rebel, a sufferer.

How can we know that God loves the world? We can know it because of a great event in history—Calvary! Does the smallness of our earth make it hard for you to believe that God loves the world? Look at the cross! Does the presence of suffering on every hand make it hard for you to believe that God loves the world? Look at the cross! We know that God loves us because of what He did. Paul says, "God demonstrated his love toward us in that while we were yet sinners Christ died for us." John says, "In this was manifested the love of God toward us because God sent his only begotten Son into the world that we might live through him." We know that God loves the world because, in the miracle of incarnation, that miracle of humility, God came in the Person of Jesus Christ to seek and to save the lost. We know that God loves the world because in the miracle of atonement that miracle of love, God, in the Person of Jesus Christ, offered His life as a ransom and shed His own blood on Calvary's hill that "whosoever believeth in him should not perish but have everlasting life." The message of John 3:16 can be trusted because it is true.

Martin Luther was troubled during his last illness by very severe headaches. Somebody suggested that he try an expensive medicine to see if he could secure a little relief. Luther smiled at the suggestion and said, "No, my best prescription for head and heart is that 'God so loved the world that he gave his only begotten Son, that whosoever believeth in him should not perish, but have everlasting life.'" This scripture is also the best prescription for a troubled heart. Bring all your doubts, all your sins, all your agonies to Calvary, and there by faith receive into your souls the Crucified Christ, and go away with your head satisfied and your heart at peace.

Creation or Chance?

The fool hath said in his heart, There is no God.
PSALM 14:1

HOW WOULD THE PSALMIST express himself if he were alive today, when unbelief is no longer confined to the secret recesses of the heart, but is blatantly published abroad in the name of reason, enlightenment, and progress? Atheism is folly, as the Psalmist said; and the world is full of fools. Some of them, it must be admitted, are very highly educated and intelligent.

Consider this statement by Robert Blatchford, the most powerful journalist in England a generation ago:

> I claim that the heavenly Father is a myth; that in face of a knowledge of life and the world, we cannot reasonably believe in Him. There is no heavenly Father watching tenderly over us, His children. He is the baseless shadow of a wistful human dream.
>
> I do not believe in a God. The belief in a God is still generally accepted. . . . But, in the light of scientific discoveries and demonstrations, such a belief is unfounded and utterly untenable today.

18

Consider, further, this catechism of unbelief published by the American Association for the Advancement of Atheism.

1.—Q. What is God?
A. God is an imaginary character—a myth—a creation of fiction believed by idolaters to be a real being that created and governs all things.
2.—Q. Is there a real God?
A. The universe contains no real God.
3.—Q. What is the soul?
A. The soul is an imaginary character believed by idolaters to live in people and at their death to leave them and take all their senses, mind and knowledge, and live on forever.
4.—Q. Has man a soul?
A. Man contains no soul.
5.—Q. What does dying mean?
A. Dying means the ceasing forever of all organs of the body to perform their functions.
6.—Q. What is death?
A. Death is the name of the condition or state of an organism when life ceases.
7.—Q. Will dead people ever come to life again?
A. Dead people will never come to life again.

Now these gainsayers of God are not stupid men at all; we admit their learning and intelligence. Yet, in spite of that, I insist that the language of the Psalmist is none too strong when he declares, "The fool hath said in his heart, There is no God." You see, the man who refuses to believe in a Creator must believe that everything in the world, including himself, has come into existence by pure chance. But to believe that requires much more credulity than to believe in God. That was why Francis Bacon, whose writings laid the foundation for modern science, observed in one of his famous essays, "I had rather believe all the fables in the Legend, and the Talmud, and the Alcoran, than that this universal frame is without a Mind."

Talk about miracles! The atheist must believe in a miracle which is altogether illogical and incredible. He must believe that this universe with all its orderliness, with all its intricate arrangements, all its beauty, all its machine-like functioning—the steady circling of the planets over-head, the unfaltering rotation of the stars which never deviate a hair's breadth from their courses, the march of the seasons with autumn following summer, winter fol-lowing autumn, spring following winter, year in and year out—all of this he must believe is not the product of infinite intelligence and wisdom and power, but the result of pure chance.

If a watch cannot be explained except by a creative mind, what are we to think of the man who argues that the universe can be explained apart from the creative mind of God? Truly, "The fool hath said in his heart, There is no God."

Suppose I were to take you to the Hayden Planetarium in New York City, and, awe-stricken, we were to watch its fascinating reproduction of the steady, unwearied, never-changing movement of the immense stars which constitute our universe; and suppose, after it was all over, I were to remark casually, "Of course, you know this planetarium was not planned and put together. It all just happened. One morning the citizens of New York awoke and to their surprise found it here like a mushroom that had sprung up overnight." What would be your reaction to that? I suspect you would be either very angry or very sad; either your intelligence would be insulted or else you would be overwhelmed with pity for my idiocy.

Yet remember that a planetarium is after all only a copy of the universe around us. Remember, too, that man did not think it all up and plan it all by himself; he did nothing but copy the original already in existence. And remember, furthermore, that it took all the ingenuity and resources of modern science even to make that copy. And remember, in addition, that the copy does not function automatically; it must be looked after regularly. Yet if we cannot explain the planetarium apart from human intelligence and ingenuity, how apart from divine intelligence and ingenuity can we explain the universe of which the planetarium is but a copy? Surely the Psalmist was not amiss in the curt judgment which he passed upon the atheist, "The fool hath said in his heart, There is no God."

Pure chance or personal creation, one or the other of these is responsible for our law-abiding universe concerning which F. R. Moulton of the University of Chicago makes this comment:

> To an astronomer, the most remarkable thing about the universe is not its immense size, its great age, or even the violence of forces operating within its boundaries. The thing which strikes an astronomer with awe is the element of perfect orderliness. From the tiny satellites of our solar system to the vast galaxies far beyond our own there is no trace of confusion. There is nothing haphazard, nothing capricious. The orderliness of the universe is the supreme discovery of science.

Now, what is responsible for our orderly universe, pure chance or personal creation? Only a fool will accept the explanation of pure chance. As a businessman with a keen mind wrote several years ago in the *American Magazine*:

> It takes a girl in our factory about two days to learn to put the seventeen parts of a meat chopper together. It may be that these millions of worlds, each with its separate orbit, all balanced so wonderfully in space—it may be that they just happened; it may be that by a billion years of tumbling about they finally arranged themselves. I don't know. I am merely a plain manufacturer of cutlery. But this I do know, that you can shake the seventeen parts of a meat chopper around in a washtub for the next seventeen billion years and you'll never have a meat chopper.

Everything about us points with overwhelming force to a personal Creator whose mind and power are infinite. Dr. George Gallup, whose experience as the director of nationwide polls lends authority to his opinion, declares: "I could prove God statistically. Take the human body alone. The chance that all the functions of the individual would just happen is a statistical monstrosity." Sir James Jeans, probably the greatest physicist of our time, affirms, "We discover that the universe shows evidences of a designing or controlling power that has something in common with our own individual minds." Physicist Dr. Robert Millikan, winner of the Nobel prize, declares, "To me it is unthinkable that a real atheist could be a scientist." Dr. C. A. Chant, professor of Astrophysics in Toronto University, expresses himself in this way: "I have no hesitation in saying that at least ninety per cent of astronomers have reached the conclusion that the universe is not the result of blind law, but is regulated by a great Intelligence. Slowly but surely the mind of the great is returning to the Creator and God of Providence." Everything about us points to God so overwhelmingly that only a fool can be an atheist.

If you have been denying God, may I give you some pointed advice? Stop being a fool! There *is* a God, a God with whom it is folly to trifle, a God with whom you must some day reckon. Stop denying God and instead do as Job counsels, "Acquaint now thyself with him and be at peace." If you have never before believed and if you are really a sincere seeker after truth, pray this prayer: "O God, if there be a God, reveal Thyself to me for Jesus' sake." Try that. I assure you that it works. The living God never fails to disclose Himself to a heart that truly seeks Him.

The Difficulties of Disbelief

DO YOU FIND IT HARD to believe in God? Perhaps you have been reading the daily reports from the battlefronts of the world, reports which depress because their cold statistics hint at carnage and human suffering. And perhaps, pondering on those reports, you have thought to yourself, "How can a world where bloody war is possible be the creation of a loving God? Maybe there isn't any God after all!" Or perhaps you have been visiting a friend who is dying of an incurable disease which slowly, horribly, agonizingly, eats away his body. And perhaps, visiting that friend, you have thought to yourself, "How can a world where cancer is possible be the creation of a loving God? Maybe there isn't any God after all!" Or, yet again, perhaps you have been brooding over your own life with its wrecked hopes, its repeated frustrations, its monotony and misery. And perhaps, brooding in that way, you have thought to yourself, "How can a world where a life like mine is possible be the creation of a loving God? Maybe there isn't any God after all!"

Suppose, then, finding it hard to believe in God, you decide to abandon faith and to exile the thought of God from your mind. Here, for example, related in his own words, is the experience of George Romanes, the famous English scientist, when temporarily abandoning all belief, he embraced atheism:

> I am not ashamed to confess that, with this virtual negation of God, the universe to me has lost its soul of loveliness; and although from henceforth the precept "to work while it is day" will doubtless but gain intensified force from the terribly intensified meaning of the words, "The night cometh when no man can work," yet, when at times I think, as think at times I must, of the appalling contrast between the hallowed glory of that creed which once was mine, and the lonely mystery of existence as I now find it, I shall ever feel it impossible to avoid the sharpest pang of which my nature is susceptible.

Giving up his faith in God did not help George Romanes at all. A few years ago a student at Yale University committed suicide. When his father, a distinguished writer, was asked for an explanation by the newspaper reporters, this was what he told them:

> My son saw no reason in life, and so none for it. All of us today do not know what the reason for life is. We do not understand life. Anyone who pretends to is bluffing.

Apart from God, therefore, life has no peace, no joy, no purpose, no reason.

Putting God out of the picture, how can you possibly account for the existence of the world itself? Oh, I know that very often it is lightly assumed that the world has always been and always will be. But whoever assumes that is mistaken. For modern science teaches, and teaches with a note of positiveness, that our world has not been in existence forever. What is it that Professor P. G. Tait and Balfour Stewart say in their book, *The Unseen Universe*? "It is perfectly certain . . . that the visible universe must have had its beginning in time." And again they say, "We do not hesitate to assert that the visible universe . . . had its beginning in time and will also come to an end."

And what does Sir James Jeans, the master of contemporary physicists, have to say?

> Everything points with overwhelming force to a definite event, or series of events, of creation at some time or times not infinitely remote. The universe cannot have originated by chance of its present ingredients and neither can it have always been the same as now.

If you decide to renounce all faith in a Creator of Love, another mystery emerges. How can you account not alone for the existence of the world around you but also for your own existence? Face that mystery honestly, and I am confident you will finally agree that God is the one satisfactory explanation of your existence. For here you are, put together in such a way that you can reason and reflect. You have a mind and you possess intelligence. But where did your mind come from? What was the origin of your intelligence? Is it simply the accidental outcome of a blind process of evolution? To be sure, it is very commonly said nowadays that in the beginning there was no God; instead there was nothing except water and dirt; and the primeval mud became dissatisfied with its lowly lot, and so through numberless eons lifted itself higher and higher from fish to reptiles, from reptiles to birds, from birds to animals, and at long last from animals to man with the strange power of thought. Therefore everything in the world, including even the human mind, can be explained quite easily in terms of evolving mud. Just give mud enough time and it will produce all by itself the dramas of Shakespeare, the music of Handel, the paintings of Michelangelo, and the teachings of Jesus Christ! God is not needed to interpret man and the world. Not at all! Mud and time are a sufficient explanation.

Now why such nonsense is unquestionably accepted as being the essence of truth is to me a dark enigma. Mud and time—what an explanation! Put a lump of mud in a jar on your pantry shelf, and what will happen to it? Will it ever, all of itself, become a tulip, or a dog, or a human mind? Never! Not in a hundred million years! What nonsense! If that mud is ever going to be anything else except mud, some outside force must act upon it. And so, if in a world of mud, living creatures with minds put in their appearance, it is not because mud has transformed itself but because an Eternal Mind outside the world has made those creatures in His image and likeness, equipping them with minds like unto His own. Sit where you are and think about that, and every thought will cry out, "God!"

Or take the conscience which you possess, however hotly some of the psychologists deny its existence. Here you are with a sense of *ought* from which you cannot escape. Here you are with a feeling of pride if you do certain things, and with a feeling of guilt if you do certain other things. Here you are with an idea of right and wrong. Here you are, in short, with a conscience, a unique possession. A stone does not have it. A tree has no sense of *ought*. A frog has no haunting feeling of responsibility.

A cow has no idea of right and wrong. A dog steals a link of sausage and suffers no remorse, but you cheat anyone and you are inwardly troubled and self-condemned. Now how do you account for that invisible monitor within yourself unless you admit that behind the universe is an Eternal Righteousness, a God who in creating man endowed him with a conscience to serve as a reminder that a human being is not a mere animal but a moral creation made in the very image of his Creator? Believe in God and you can explain yourself. Deny God and your own conscience will remain a perpetual mystery.

I think you will agree that the thing for you to do is not to renounce all belief because life has its ugly and puzzling aspects; rather, you should press on in your spiritual experience until you come to know God in a way so real, so vital, so personal, that never again under any circumstance will your faith in Him be on the verge of collapse. You need to know God as He has revealed Himself in and through Jesus Christ, and especially in and through Calvary's cross.

Early in this century, Robert Blatchford, of Great Britain, was editing the *Clarion,* an influential magazine in Great Britain, the sole purpose of which was the destruction of Christianity and the overthrow of all religion. A genius in the field of journalism, Blatchford made such statements as this: "There is no heavenly father watching over us, His children. He is but the baseless shadow of a wistful human dream. . . . If God were a God of love, He would not choose to create a world in which hate and pain should have a place. Why does He permit pain and hate to continue?" It was so hard for Robert Blatchford to believe in God that he was an atheist, defying and denying

Deity. But when his wife died, that unbelieving editor found that it was harder not to believe in God than to believe in Him. Let me quote from his autobiography:

> When I got up on the morning of her death I found to my surprise that I did not believe that she was dead. My materialism notwithstanding I felt that my wife was alive. My daughter, who held the same materialistic views as I did, felt the same. We could not believe that she was not.

Robert Blatchford discovered that he needed the God whom he had defied and denied with all his powers. He cried out to God for pardon in the name of Jesus Christ and learned how divinely true is the precious promise of Scripture, "Him that cometh unto me I will in no wise cast out." And as he came to his journey's end, he confessed, "I will not dissemble nor cloak my sins, but . . . I can repeat without blushing the golden sentence, 'That it may please Thee, O God, to strengthen such as do stand; and to comfort and help the weak-hearted; and to raise up them that fall.'"

Come to God in the name of Jesus, confessing that you are a blinded, bewildered sinner. Come, beseeching Him to grant you sight and light; and He will hear you and help you and draw you into a fellowship which fills both life and death with heavenly glory.

Liar, Lunatic, or Lord of All?

JUDGED BY HUMAN STANDARDS of success, the life of Jesus Christ was a pathetic failure. Born in a manger, He was buried in a borrowed grave. His family was poor, and for thirty years He lived in an obscure village of Palestine working as a carpenter. His own brothers thought He was mad and tried to dissuade Him when He started out to preach. His teachings were hated and scoffed at by theologians of that day. Some of His followers came from the lowest level of society. His intimate friends misunderstood Him and in the end, like cowards, let Him die alone at the hand of His enemies. He never wrote a book. He never commanded an army. He never addressed a senate or spoke to an applauding parliament. He never occupied a throne. At the age of thirty-three He perished in torture and disgrace, nailed up against the sky between two thieves.

Yet Jesus Christ spoke about Himself in a way that is simply astonishing. He asserted that He was a teacher whose doctrines should be accepted unquestioningly; that He was the perfect example of human character and conduct; that He was an absolutely sinless Being; that He was able to work miracles such as no other man had ever wrought; that He would rise from the dead; that He would be the final Judge of the world; that He was equal with God in power and authority. Indeed, He even asserted that He was God! Yes, He commanded His disciples to love Him, obey Him, follow Him, sacrifice for Him, believe in Him, worship Him and, if need be, die for Him exactly as they would for God.

Now in the light of these assertions, what are we to think concerning Jesus Christ? Faced as you are with these amazing claims and all their implications, what is your opinion regarding Him? One thing at least you must admit, as every reflecting man is compelled to do: This strange Carpenter of Galilee who somehow steps across twenty centuries and breaks into our lives even today, cannot be pushed to one side as a profound teacher and nothing more; or a courageous martyr and nothing more; or a religious genius and nothing more. For if Jesus was and is really God as He claimed to be, you cannot with knowing condescension dismiss Him as a mere teacher or a mere martyr or a mere genius. To dismiss God in that way is blasphemy! If He really was and is Deity incarnate, you must fall before Him in adoring faith and love and surrender. On the other hand, however, if Jesus Christ was not and is not really God as He claimed to be, how can you possibly look upon Him admiringly as the noblest example of the good life, a life of unselfish humility and lowly service? If His claim is false, you must agree that this Galilean Carpenter was either a liar or a lunatic. Certainly! Of necessity He must have been one or the other if He was not Deity incarnate.

Now, which was He? A liar? Is *that* what He was? Not according to David Strauss, the world-renowned German scholar. Listen to the opinion of this man who was far from being a Christian:

> He represents within the religious sphere the highest point, beyond which posterity cannot go; yea, whom it cannot even equal, inasmuch as everyone who hereafter should climb the same height, could only do it with the help of Jesus, who first attained it. As little as humanity will ever be without religion, as little will it be without Christ; for to have religion without Christ would be as absurd as to enjoy poetry without regard to Homer or Shakespeare. . . . He remains the highest model of religion within the reach of our thought; and no perfect piety is possible without His presence in the heart.

Nor was Jesus Christ a liar in the opinion of Theodore Parker, the distinguished American Unitarian.

> That mightiest heart that ever beat, stirred by the spirit of God, how it wrought in His bosom! What words of rebuke, of comfort, counsel, admonition, promise, hope, did He pour out! words that stir the soul as summer dews call up the faint and sickly grass. What profound instruction in His proverbs and discourses! What wisdom in His homely sayings, so rich with Jewish life! What deep divinity of soul in His prayers, His actions, sympathy, resignation! Try Him as we try other teachers. They deliver their words; find a few waiting for the consolation, who accept the new tidings, follow the new method, and soon go beyond their teacher, though less mighty minds than he. But eighteen centuries have passed since the tide of humanity rose so high in Jesus: what man, what sect, what church, has mastered His thought, comprehended His method, and so fully applied it to life?

Let the world answer in its cry of anguish. Men have parted His raiment among them, cast lots for His seamless coat; but that spirit which toiled so manfully in a world of sin and death, which died and suffered and overcame the world, — is that found, possessed, understood!

Well, then, if Jesus was not a liar, was He a lunatic? Was He a deluded fanatic? George Bernard Shaw, to whom nothing and nobody was sacred, ventured to assert that Jesus is "a man who was sane until Peter hailed Him as the Christ and who then became a monomaniac. . . . His delusion is a very common delusion among the insane and . . . such insanity is quite consistent with the retention of the argumentative cunning and penetration which Jesus displayed in Jerusalem after His delusion had taken complete hold of Him." But was Jesus Christ really a lunatic? William E. Channing, another famous Unitarian, has this to say in that regard:

> The charge of self-deluding fanaticism is the last to be fastened on Jesus. Where can we find traces of it in His history? Do we detect them in the calm authority of His precepts; in the mild, practical, beneficent spirit of His religion; in the simplicity of the language in which He unfolds His high powers and the sublime truths of religion; or in the good sense, the knowledge of human nature which He always discloses in His estimate and treatment of the different classes of men with whom He acted? . . . The truth is that remarkable as was the character of Jesus, it was distinguished by nothing more than by calmness and self-possession.

Moreover, if we can trust the judgment of William

Lecky, one of the most noted historians of Great Britain, Jesus Christ was not a lunatic. Here is what Lecky writes:

> It was reserved for Christianity to present to the world an ideal character which through all the changes of eighteen centuries has inspired the hearts of men with an impassioned love; has shown itself capable of acting on all ages, nations, temperaments and conditions; has been not only the highest pattern of virtue, but the strongest incentive to its practice. . . . The simple record of these three short years of active life has done more to regenerate and soften mankind than all the disquisitions of philosophers and all the exhortations of moralists.

Was Jesus a lunatic? Not according to William Lecky who spent his life in an attempt to destroy organized Christianity!

And if you are still in doubt as to this point, consider these words of John Stuart Mill, one of the keenest philosophers of modern times:

> About the life and sayings of Jesus there is a stamp of personal originality combined with profundidity of insight, which must place the prophet of Nazareth, even in the estimation of those who have no belief in his inspiration, in the very first rank of the men of sublime genius of whom our species can boast. When this pre-eminent genius is combined with the qualities of probably the greatest moral reformer, and martyr to that mission, who ever existed upon earth, religion cannot be said to have made a bad choice in picking on this man as the ideal representative and guide of humanity; nor, even now would it be easy, even for an unbeliever, to find a better translation of the rule of virtue from the abstract

into concrete, than to endeavor so to live that Christ would approve our life.

And John Stuart Mill, like William Lecky, had little use for Christianity.

Whenever anybody seriously argues with me that Jesus was an extreme pathological case, I like to point out how strange it is that the most learned, cultured, critical intellects of all ages have bowed in reverent homage at the feet of this young fanatic, addressing Him as Master. And, whenever any critic insists that He was demented, I like to exclaim, "Would to God that the whole world were affected with His kind of insanity!"

Well, then, since Jesus Christ cannot be pushed aside as a liar or waved away as a lunatic, what conclusion must we draw? Jesus Christ is what He claimed to be! He is the Lord of glory, Deity incarnate, God humbling Himself to become man in order to redeem His lost creation. And since that is so, it is blasphemy for us to talk patronizingly about Him as a teacher or a martyr or a religious genius. Instead, we must fall down at His nail-pierced feet in adoration and faith, exclaiming, "My Lord and my God."

The Godlike Galilean

WHY DO Christians hold unwaveringly to the belief that Jesus was and is God? To begin with, Christians believe that Jesus of Nazareth, who lived in poverty and expired in agony, was and is Almighty God *because of His Godlike character*. He was holy and loving and righteous in all His ways. He was precisely what you might imagine God to be like if He were to lay aside His glory and live as a man among men.

This is not the opinion of Christians only; they are open to the charge of prejudice. This has also been the verdict of competent judges who made no profession of personal faith in Jesus as their Saviour. This, for instance, is the verdict of Rousseau. Comparing Socrates the Greek and Jesus the Galilean, he exclaims:

> The death of Socrates, peacefully philosophising among friends, appears the most agreeable that one could wish: that of Jesus, expiring in agonies, abused, insulted and accused by a whole nation, is the most horrible that one could fear. Socrates, indeed, in receiving the cup of poison, blessed the weeping executioneer who administered it; but Jesus, amidst excru-

36

ciating tortures, prayed for his merciless tormentors. Yes, if the life and death of Socrates were those of a sage, the life and death of Jesus are those of a God.

And that opinion is shared by many other notable world-figures, for instance, Napoleon Bonaparte. On the lonely isle of St. Helena the exiled emperor was once discussing Christ with General Bertrand, a faithful officer who had followed him into banishment and who did not believe in the Deity of Jesus. This is what Napoleon said:

> I know men; and I tell you that Jesus Christ is not a man. Superficial minds see a resemblance between Christ and the founders of empires, and the gods of other religions. That resemblance does not exist. There is between Christianity and whatever other religions the distance of infinity. . . . Everything in Christ astonishes me. His spirit overawes me, and his will confounds me. Between him and whoever else in the world, there is no possible term of comparison. He is truly a being by himself. His ideas and sentiments, the truth which he announces, his manner of convincing, are not explained either by human organization or by the nature of things. . . . The nearer I approach, the more carefully I examine, everything is above me—everything remains grand, of a grandeur which overpowers. His religion is a revelation from an intelligence which certainly is not that of man. . . . One can absolutely find nowhere, but in him alone, the imitation or the example of his life. . . . I search in vain in history to find the similar to Jesus Christ, or anything which can approach the gospel. Neither history, nor humanity, nor the ages, nor nature, offer me anything with which I am able to compare it or to explain it. Here everything is extraordinary.

For another thing, Christians believe that Jesus of Nazareth, who lived in poverty and expired in agony, was and is Almighty *God because of His Godlike teaching*. Now you must remember that this Teacher who had no place to lay His head, had no opportunity at all for the formal education which we rightly prize so highly. He never attended a grammar school, and, apart from the Old Testament, had no books at home which He might study. Neither did He have access to a library where He might become acquainted with culture and philosophy. He grew up in the midst of ignorance and bigotry and superstition and intolerance. Yet this Man gave to the world a body of teaching which up to the present hour has never been equaled, or surpassed, or even remotely approached by the greatest sages and most learned thinkers.

Consider this as a sidelight upon the amazing quality of His teaching. Fifteen years ago Arthur Hinds compiled a little book which he entitled *The Complete Sayings of Jesus*. It was a condensation of the Gospels in which the narrative was set in small type while the words of Christ were printed boldly so that they immediately attracted attention. Recently a prominent official of one of the radio networks, who says of himself that he is not "particularly religious," came across that little book and decided it was of such unusual value that it must be widely circulated; so he privately undertook the task. On the last report some twenty-five thousand copies had already been distributed. Bear in mind that it contains nothing but the Words of a Teacher of long ago who was crucified at the age of thirty-three. Dale Carnegie, author of the best seller, *How to Win Friends and Influence People,* writes about it in this way:

Lowell Thomas said to me recently: "Dale, I've just come across a little book that is the complete expression of everything we are fighting for. You'll be impressed by the book and the story behind it, and I have a hunch it would greatly interest your readers." And he sent me that extraordinary little book. It fits into the vest pocket and you can read it in a couple of hours, yet it contains every recorded word of a man who has 700,000,000 followers. Its title: *The Complete Sayings of Jesus.* If I know anything at all about human nature, many of my readers will welcome this little vest pocket book as a "find." For this is no tract primarily for the religious or the literary. It is a working manual packed with practical guidance for solving the daily problems of human relationships. More than that, it contains the teachings of the greatest of all teachers of the difference between right and wrong — which is basically the reason why we are fighting the Axis.

For still another thing, Christians believe that Jesus of Nazareth, who lived in poverty and expired in agony, was and is Almighty God *because of His Godlike influence.* Now ordinarily when a young criminal is put to death, no matter how sensational his career might have been, very speedily his memory is blotted out. But Jesus, this strange Teacher of antiquity, who was crucified at the age of thirty-three, is reported to have said to His disciples on the night of His execution, "I have overcome the world." What a preposterous statement to make when to all appearances the world had proved too much for Him and at last was to destroy Him! Nevertheless, it is a verifiable fact of history that out of the life of this strange young Man who was put to death as a criminal there has flowed the most penetrating, transforming and uplifting influence in all history. Consider this:

> Jesus of Nazareth, without money and arms, conquered more millions than Alexander, Caesar, Mohammed and Napoleon; without science and learning, He shed more light on things human and divine, than all the philosophers and scholars combined; without the eloquence of the school, He spoke words of life such as were never spoken before, nor since, and produced effects which lie beyond the reach of orator or poet; without writing a single line, He has set more pens in motion and furnished themes for more sermons, orations, discussions, works of art, learned volumes, and sweet songs of praise than the whole army of great men of ancient and modern times. Born in a manger and crucified as a malefactor, He now controls the destinies of the civilized world, and rules a spiritual empire which embraces one-third of the inhabitants of the globe.

So wrote Philip Schaff, and he was by no means exaggerating when he wrote in that fashion. Or consider this:

> Measured by its fruits in the human race, that short life has been the most influential ever lived on this planet. As we have been at pains to point out, the impress of that life, far from fading with the passing centuries, has deepened. Through Him millions of individuals have been transformed and have begun to live the kind of life which He exemplified. . . . Gauged by the consequences which have followed, the birth, life, death, and resurrection of Jesus have been the most important events in the history of man. Measured by His influence, Jesus is central in the human story.

So says Kenneth Scott Latourette, director of department of religion in Yale's graduate school, and he is not exaggerating when he says that.

The life of Jesus Christ has exerted a Godlike influence upon the world. That is why Christians believe that Jesus is God. Which is more reasonable, to believe that this Man of Godlike influence who claimed to be God was really God, or to believe that He was a liar or a lunatic?

And more than that, Christians believe that Jesus is God *because He has done and is still doing for men what only God can do.* Men have a hunger in their souls, and Jesus Christ who said "I am the bread of life" somehow satisfies man's deepest longings and yearnings; only God can do that. Men are as sheep going astray, living aimlessly and hopelessly, and He who said "I am the Good Shepherd" guides them into pathways of purposefulness and pleasure and peace; only God can do that. Men are blind to the wonder and glory of the kingdom of heaven, and He who said "I am the light" makes them see the wonder and glory of the world invisible; only God can do that. Men are entangled in error, uncertain as to the answers to the great problems of existence, and He who said "I am the truth" brings them to the place where they can look out upon life serenely and surely, affirming " We *know*"; only God can do that. Men are dead in trespasses and sins, and He who said "I am the resurrection and the life" raises them up and makes them alive to righteousness and purity and holiness; only God can do that. Men are helplessly lost and undone, and He who said "I am Jesus the Saviour" saves them and re-makes them so that they truly become new creations; and only God can do that. According to the *New York Times,* far out on an island in the Pacific an army Chaplain has built a church out of driftwood. He has taken shipwrecks which littered the island's shores and he has erected a chapel to the memory of an airman who lost his life, a chapel in which the soldiers gather to glorify God. Imagine that! A church for the glory of God, built out of shipwrecks and driftwood! But that is exactly how Jesus Christ is building His own Church. He is taking shipwrecked lives and human driftwood, and out of such material He is erecting a Church which for all eternity will be to the glory of God. Is that not proof that this man Jesus Himself is God?

A drunkard, who for many years had squandered his wages on liquor and had terribly maltreated his family and was transformingly converted, was giving his testimony one night on a street corner. A sneering skeptic began to ask him questions like this: Where was Jesus born? Who was His father? Who was His mother? How did He earn His living? And the former drunkard, totally ignorant of Scripture, was nonplused until in a flash of inspiration he replied, "I don't know anything about that; but I do know that just a few weeks ago my wife was unhappy, and my children were in want and hated me, and my own heart was in misery. But then I was saved, and now everything is different. My wife is happy; my children love me; and I have joy in my own heart. And I know that Jesus did it all!" Well, that's enough! He who does for men what only God can do must be, as He said He was, God incarnate.

> Who will open mercy's door?
> Jesus will, Jesus will;
> As for pardon I implore,
> Jesus, blessed Jesus, will!

Who will take away my sin?
   Jesus will, Jesus will;
Make me pure without, within,
   Jesus, blessed Jesus, will!

Who can conquer doubts and fears?
   Jesus will, Jesus will;
Share my joys and dry my tears,
   Jesus, blessed Jesus, will!

A Baffling Book

O Word of God incarnate!
O Wisdom from on high!
O Truth unchanged, unchanging,
O Light of our dark sky;
We praise Thee for the radiance
That from Thy hallowed page,
A lantern to our footsteps
Shines on from age to age.

W. W. How

PERHAPS YOUR CONCEPTION of the Bible is very different from that of the poet. Perhaps to you, as to Harry Elmer Barnes, the noted historian, it is "a purely secular product of human ingenuity." Although that may be your conception of the Bible, there is one thing about it to which, I am sure, you will agree: regardless of whether or not it was inspired by God, the Bible occupies a unique place among all the millions of other books that constitute the world's literature. Let us consider, then, a few of the strange and significant features of this collection of ancient Jewish writings.

Consider, first, how extraordinary it is that this collection of ancient Jewish history, poetry, and prophecy has lived on for thousands of years. That in itself is a very strange and significant fact. Hundreds of centuries have slowly ticked away since the Bible was written; a score or so of powerful civilizations have flourished, decayed, and vanished, leaving scarcely a trace of their existence; war and fire and human negligence have wiped out the records of antiquity to so large an extent that the books of such nations of antiquity as the Phoenicians and the Hittites and the Cretans are lost to us. And yet for some unaccountable reason these ancient writings of the Hebrews have survived, although by all the laws of probability they likewise should have perished. So perhaps, after all, there is something to what the Bible says when it declares in reference to itself, "The grass withereth and the flower thereof falleth away: but the word of the Lord endureth forever" (I Peter 1:24, 25).

> Century follows century—There it stands.
>
> Empires rise and fall and are forgotten—There it stands.
>
> Dynasty succeeds dynasty—There it stands.
>
> Kings are crowned and uncrowned—There it stands.
>
> Despised and torn to pieces—There it stands.
>
> Storms of hate swirl about it—There it stands.
>
> Agnostics smile cynically—There it stands.
>
> Profane, prayerless punsters caricature it—There it stands.
>
> Unbelief abandons it—There it stands.
>
> Thunderbolts of wrath smite it—There it stands.
>
> The flames are kindled about it—There it stands.
>
> The arrows of hate are discharged against it—There it stands.
>
> Radicalism rants and raves against it—There it stands.
>
> Fogs of sophistry conceal it temporarily—There it stands.

The tooth of time gnaws, but makes no dent—There
  it stands.
Modernism tries to explain it away—There it stands.
An anvil that has broken a million hammers—There
  it stands.

—A. Z. CONRAD

What is there, then, about this ancient Book which
has not only enabled it to live on through centuries of
change and decay but which has also enabled it to live
on in spite of untiring and powerful attempts to destroy
it? As Theodore Watts Dunton, one of the penetrating
critics of our time, puts it:

> A great living savant has characterized the Bible
> as "a collection of the rude imaginings of Syria,"
> "the worn-out old bottle of Judaism into which the
> generous new wine of science is being poured." The
> great savant was mad when he said so. The "new
> wine" of science is a generous vintage, undoubtedly,
> and deserves all the respect it gets from us; so do those
> who make it and serve it out; they have so much intel-
> ligence; they are so honest and fearless. But whatever
> may become of their wine in a few years, when the
> wine-dealers shall have passed away, when the savant
> is forgotten as any stargazer of Chaldea—the "old bot-
> tle" is going to be older yet—the Bible is going to be
> eternal.

Why is it that nearly one billion Bibles have been
circulated since in 1448 Johann Gutenberg of Germany
turned out the first printed copy of Scripture? Why has
this Book, produced in a remote corner of the Orient,
been translated out of its "dead" languages into more than
one thousand living tongues and dialects? And why is it
that, unlike the classics, it is studied and treasured and

loved not only by scholars but by multitudes of common folk in every circumstance and station of life?

Why is it that, when in 1881 the revision of the New Testament was about to be issued, wealthy men offered five thousand dollars to secure one in advance; and as Dr. William Biederwolf relates, "On the morning it was published the streets of New York City were blockaded with scores of express wagons waiting for copies of the Book which infidels had exploded and refuted and killed and buried so many years before"? Why is it that Generalissimo Chiang Kai-Shek and his wife regard it as a necessity to rise daily at 5:30 to peruse this ancient Book before busying themselves with their staggering responsibilities? Why is it that, when Henry Stanley journeyed into the tangled forest of Africa to find David Livingstone, he started out with one hundred-eighty pounds of books, but as hunger and illness forced the sacrifice of unessentials he discarded volume after volume until all he had left was an edition of Shakespeare, a copy of Carlyle, two treatises on navigation, and the Bible; and concerning these five books he said on his return to the United States, "Poor Shakespeare was afterwards burned up; Carlyle and the navigation books were abandoned by the way, and I had only the Bible left"? And during that expedition, mind you, he read his Bible through three times; and here is how he, a sophisticated man of the world, describes what that reading did to him and for him.

> During my first attack of African fever, I took up the Bible to while away tedious hours. I read Job, and then the Psalms. The Bible, with its noble and simple language, I continued to read with a higher and truer understanding than I had ever before con-

ceived. Its powerful verses had a different meaning, a more penetrative influence, in the silence of the wilds. I came to feel a strange glow while absorbed in its pages, and a charm peculiarly appropriate to the deep melancholy of African scenery. When I laid down the book, the mind commenced to feed upon what memory suggested. Then rose the ghosts of bygone yearnings, haunting every cranny of the brain with numbers of baffled hopes and unfulfilled aspirations. . . . Alone in my tent, I flung myself on my knees, and poured out my soul utterly in secret prayer to Him from whom I had been so long estranged; to Him who had led me here mysteriously into Africa, there to reveal Himself, and His will. I became then inspired with fresh desire to serve Him to the utmost, that same desire which in early days in New Orleans filled me each morning, and sent me joyfully skipping to my work.

Why is it that Captain Paul Riggs, after drifting alone on the Pacific Ocean for one hundred fifteen days, bore this testimony: "I read the Bible through twice. I had a few novels with me but didn't touch them. The Bible kept me sane"? Why is it that Dr. Charles Eliot, one of the most learned men of recent times, as he lay dying in his ninety-second year, read the Old Testament again for the last of a score of times; and, when one morning his daughter asked him what he was doing, exclaimed, "I am reading news!"? Why is it that Dr. Howard A. Kelly, professor of gynecology at Johns Hopkins University, a scientist of international repute, made it his practice never to read anything but the Bible every day after supper? Why is it that an industrial wizard like Henry Ford always carried a portion of this ancient Book with him, and why is it that, when celebrating his birthday on July 30, he stated to the newspaper reporters who interviewed him, "The Bible does not need advertising by me, but I wish more people could be persuaded to read the Bible"? What is there, then, about this Book, I ask once more, which endows it with a perennial appeal and a universal fascination? Say what you will, the Bible is certainly very extraordinary.

And, in addition, consider how this collection of ancient writings is venerated and respected even today by outstanding thinkers. How strange it is that the Hebrews, considered by many as superstitious, should have produced the Book which continues to be the moral standard and guide for the modern world! What a significant fact that is! So President Faunce of Brown University declared:

> Not one of you would think of looking in a book of medicine which was published fifty years ago; not one of you would think of using a compendium of science fifty years old; not one of you would think of taking as authoritative the statements in a book on psychology that was even twenty years old. Mr. Wells' *Outline of History* had to be revised even before it was published. Here is a Book which remains the standard guide of the world after all these centuries.

So, too, Admiral Alfred T. Mahan in an address to the cadets at West Point affirmed:

> After much experience of bad and good, of religion and irreligion, I assure you with the full force of the conviction of a lifetime, that to one who has mastered the Word of God, even imperfectly, it brings a light, a motive, a strength, and a support which nothing else does.

So, also, author Charles Dickens, when his youngest son was leaving home to join a brother in Australia, said to him in a letter:

> I put a New Testament among your books for the very same reasons, and with the very same hopes, that made me write an easy account of it for you, when you were a little child. Because it is the best book that ever was, or will be, known in the world; and because it teaches you the best lessons by which any human creature, who tries to be truthful and faithful to duty, can possibly be guided. As your brothers have gone away, one by one, I have written to each such words as I am now writing to you, and have entreated them all to guide themselves by this Book, putting aside the interpretations and inventions of man.

Now what is there about this very ancient Book, produced by a "superstitious" race, which makes it the moral guide and standard for the modern world? Say what you will about the Bible, it is certainly very extraordinary.

Indeed, this Book is so extraordinary that it is the one Book which you simply cannot afford to neglect. If you do, the time may come when you will lament as Patrick Henry did on his deathbed:

> Here is a Book worth more than all the others ever printed; yet it is my misfortune never to have found time to read it. It is now too late. I trust in the mercy of God.

Why not begin to read this extraordinary Book today? Do not gullibly accept the negations and sneers of unbelief but see for yourself whether or not this extraordinary Book is what it professes to be, the revelation of the eternal God. Open your Bible and you will have an experience similar to that of Vido Mati, a student of Barcelona, Spain. Working on a thesis for his doctorate, he ransacked the University library for the writings of Hierro, an obscure Spanish thinker of the eighteenth century who has been generally neglected. After a long search he unearthed a dusty volume of Hierro and in turning the pages came across a document written by the old philosopher in 1741. It was Hierro's will, bequeathing all his worldly goods to the first man who would study this book which he apparently surmised would be ignored by his unappreciative countrymen. The Spanish courts declared that the will was legal and Vido Mati collected nearly two hundred-fifty thousand dollars.

That ancient and neglected Bible which you have in your possession contains an even more priceless will than the one discovered by Vido Mati. It contains the title-deeds to eternal life, signed and sealed by the blood of Calvary's Cross.

Prophetic Proof

NO HUMAN BEING has the power to predict with certainty precisely what will take place next year, or next month, or next week, or even tomorrow. Of course, he may hazard a guess regarding the probable pattern of his own life; and, if he has an adequate knowledge of history and a thorough understanding of present tendencies, he may also hazard a guess as to the outworking of affairs in the world at large. But he cannot foretell with any assurance or definiteness just what will occur. Only omniscience can prophesy accurately, and omniscience belongs only to God.

For example, on November 29, 1943, the *New Republic* put out a bulletin entitled, "America and the Postwar World," in which this statement was made: "While prophecy is dangerous, on the law of averages it is safe to predict that our relations with the rest of the world would be better under a continuing Democratic administration than under a Republican." Now that statement is significant not because of the political opinion expressed, but because it is a revealing admission of human inability to foretell the future. The writers of that article, who are among the keenest minds in America, in confessing that "prophecy is dangerous" admit that no man, however well-informed, can be certain what will take place on the tomorrows which have yet to dawn.

And for confirmation of those confessions, consider this forecast made by Norvell, the popular astrologer of Hollywood, printed (notice the date) in *Look* magazine, November 21, 1939: "In a matter of months Hitler will meet a tragic fate. Death may come to him from an assassin, or by a battle wound in the throat or heart region, or even by suicide. His end will be sudden and violent amidst much confusion. The Spring of 1940 is the period of worst affliction in Hitler's chart but in any event he cannot survive the year." Norvell also predicted, "With the Maginot Line as an impregnable barrier, England and France will invade German Territory, weakening Germany and at last shattering her morale." Norvell very palpably was guessing, not foretelling.

The Bible claims to be a revelation of the plans and purposes of the omniscient Creator. Certainly that claim cannot be contemptuously ignored; it must be carefully investigated. For if that claim is indeed backed by fulfilled prophecy, Christianity has every right to assert that the Bible is the Word of the living God; and, on the other hand, no skeptical unbeliever has the intellectual or moral right to deny that the Bible is the Word of the living God unless he is able to demonstrate that its prophecies are unfounded guesses. The famous British soldier, Marshall Wade, laughed at the Christian belief that the Bible is a divine revelation until Bishop Newton, a learned scholar, showed him that several of its prophecies had been specifically fulfilled. Whereupon in amazement the Marshall declared: "If this point can be proved to satisfaction, there will be no argument against such plain matter of fact; it will certainly convince me, and I believe it will be the readiest way to convince every reasonable man of the truth of revelation." Can this point, then, be proved to satisfaction? Is the Bible truly the Word of the living God? Does it contain fulfilled prophecy? Today let me confine myself to a single illustration, the history of the Jews.

First, centuries ago it was predicted that, because of their disobedience to God, the Israelites would be universally scattered.

> The Lord shall cause thee to be smitten before thine enemies: thou shalt go out one way against them, and flee seven days before them: and shalt be removed into all the kingdoms of the earth.
>
> *Deuteronomy 28:25*

> And the Lord shall scatter thee among all people, from the one end of the earth even unto the other; and there thou shalt serve other gods, which neither thou nor thy fathers have known, even wood and stone.
>
> *Deuteronomy 28:64*

> My God will cast them away, because they did not hearken unto him: and they shall be wanderers among the nations.
>
> *Hosea 9:17*

The Hebrews, who anciently inhabited Palestine, have been uprooted from their homeland and dispersed to every point of the compass. But how were Moses and Hosea able to foretell the future unless the omniscient God revealed it to them?

Second, centuries ago it was predicted that the Jews, exiled among the Gentiles, would be objects of contempt and terms of derision.

> And thou shalt become an astonishment, a pro-verb, and a by-word, among all nations whither the Lord shall lead thee.
>
> *Deuteronomy 28:37*

> And I will deliver them to be removed into all the kingdoms of the earth for their hurt, to be a reproach and a proverb, a taunt and a curse, in all places whither I shall drive them.
>
> *Jeremiah 24:9*

Explain them as you will, these predictions have been fulfilled; and though we deplore using the name of a race with a glorious heritage as a taunt and a curse, we admit that it is done.

Third, centuries ago it was predicted that Israel would be horribly hounded and brutally persecuted.

> And among these nations shalt thou find no ease, neither shall the sole of thy foot have rest: but the Lord shall give thee there a trembling heart, and failing of eyes, and sorrow of mind:
> And thy life shall hang in doubt before thee; and thou shalt fear day and night, and shalt have none assurance of thy life:
> In the morning thou shalt say, Would God it were even! and at even thou shalt say, Would God it were morning! for the fear of thine heart where-with thou shalt fear, and for the sight of thine eyes which thou shalt see.
>
> *Deuteronomy 28:65-67*

The history of the Jew down through the ages verifies the literal truth of this prophecy. And in our day its truth has been verified again by the ghastly pogroms of Nazi Germany.

Fourth, centuries ago it was predicted that the troubles of Israel would not be of brief duration but would be indefinitely prolonged. So Moses wrote:

> The Lord will make thy plagues wonderful, and the plagues of thy seed, even great plagues, and of long continuance, and sore sicknesses, and of long continuance.
>
> *Deuteronomy 28:59*

"Of long continuance"—that was the prophecy regarding the sufferings and sorrows of Abram's seed. And thus it has been: year in, year out, the innocent Jew has been the scapegoat of the Western civilization. Hounded by Babylonians, Persians, and Greeks, he was hounded even more by imperial Rome, and by Christian Rome— oh, the tragedy of it!—even more viciously still. During the Middle Ages he was treated as an animal rather than a human being. And in modern times, despite the humanitarianism on which we pride ourselves, he has been mercilessly hounded as never before. God grant that in this boasted "land of the free" we shall have the decency and charity and justice never to permit such outrages to occur!

Fifth, centuries ago Jeremiah announced:

> Thus saith the Lord, which giveth the sun for a light by day, and the ordinances of the moon and of the stars for a light by night, which divideth the sea when the waves thereof roar; the Lord of hosts is his name:

> If those ordinances depart from before me, saith the Lord, then the seed of Israel also shall cease from being a nation before me forever.
>
> *Jeremiah 31:35-36*

> Fear thou not, O Jacob my servant, saith the Lord: for I am with thee; for I will make a full end of all the nations whither I have driven thee: but I will not make a full end of thee, but correct thee in measure; yet will I not leave thee wholly unpunished.
>
> *Jeremiah 46:28*

God has made a full end of the Chaldeans, and the Babylonians. The Edomites are gone; the Ammonites have completely disappeared. But where are the Hebrews? They are still with us! As Dean Milman put it in his great *History of the Jews*:

> Their perpetuity, their national immortality, is at once the most curious problem to the political student and to the religious man a subject of profound and awful admiration.

Likewise, Disraeli, himself a Jew, once wrote:

> The attempt to extirpate them has been made under the most favorable auspices and on the largest scale; the most considerable means that man could command have been pertinaciously applied to this object for the longest period of recorded time. Egyptian pharaohs, Assyrian kings, Roman emperors, Scandinavian crusaders, Gothic princes, and holy inquisitors, have alike devoted their energies to the fulfillment of this common purpose. Expatriation, exile, captivity, confiscation, torture on the most ingenious, and massacre on the most extensive scale, a curious

system of degrading customs and debasing laws which would have broken the heart of any other people, have been tried, and in vain.

Sixth, centuries ago it was predicted that the Jews, scattered among foreign nations, would manage to retain their identity and remain a separate people. In the Book of Ezekiel you have that forecast in these words:

> And that which cometh into your mind shall not be at all, that ye say, We will be as the heathen, as the families of the countries, to serve wood and stone.
>
> *Ezekiel 20:32*

Only omniscience can foretell the future; and if there are genuine prophecies and fulfillments in the Bible which claims to be the Word of God, what conclusion follows? The Bible must be accepted for what it claims to be. It must be a revelation of the plans and purposes of the all-knowing Creator. But, if that is so, then another conclusion follows: When the Bible declares "All have sinned," that statement must be accepted. When the Bible declares "The wages of sin is death," that statement must be accepted. When the Bible declares "Christ died for our sins, the Just for the unjust that he might bring us to God," that statement must be accepted. When the Bible declares "Believe on the Lord Jesus Christ and thou shalt be saved," that statement must be accepted. Then why not believe in Him and by your own experience verify the Bible's truth?

Stones Speak Up

SEVERAL YEARS AGO the *Saturday Evening Post* carried a very interesting story entitled *Battle by Bible*. Listen to what its author, John Hix, has to say:

They tell this one to the men at the Army's Command and General Staff School at Fort Leavenworth, Kansas, these days—the strange incident in which the Bible supplied not merely inspiration, but a precise plan of battle, to the British in the Near East under General Allenby, in 1918.

The British, out to capture Jericho, knew they must first eliminate a Turkish garrison at the village of Michmash. A frontal attack was decided upon, despite the heavy casualties it would inevitably entail. What happened after that constitutes one of the most unusual episodes in military annals.

On February thirteenth, the eve of the attack, the British chief of staff outlined to his officers the plan for taking Michmash by direct assault. One of the officers, Major Petrie, started inwardly. The name of the village was familiar to him. After the meeting Petrie retired to his quarters to try to sleep. But the word "Michmash" kept running through his brain. Where had he encountered it? Suddenly he had the answer—the Book of Samuel, in the Bible. Quickly he located the passages he wanted, in Samuel I, chapters 13 and 14. Petrie rushed to the quarters of the commanding officer. Rousing him from sleep, he excitedly announced his find.

It was the Biblical account of how Jonathan had taken Michmash from the Philistines nearly thirty centuries before. Various landmarks were mentioned; two sharp rocks which indicated a pass; a plot of ground overlooking the town. On a hunch, the commander sent scouts out to look for the landmarks. They returned with the report that they were all there.

That night Petrie and the commander pored over the Biblical passages and completely changed the British plan of attack. Just before daybreak a small force set out for the plot of ground above Michmash. At dawn they emerged from hiding, with loud cries. The Turks poured from their huts, saw the men on the strategic ledge behind them. Confused and terrorized, they were easily subdued. Michmash was taken with amazingly few casualties, and the door to the Near East opened for a great British victory.

Now, of course, such accuracy in a very ancient collection of writings may rather surprise you. But to a Christian, accuracy of that kind is precisely what one ought to find in the Bible, since it is more than just a book which has come down to us from remote times: in his opinion it is the Word of the living God. And, consequently, he is not startled when, as in the capture of Michmash during World War I, its uncanny reliability is vividly illustrated. He knows that God is altogether true, and therefore, cannot be the Author of falsehood. And so he reasons that if the Bible has indeed been divinely inspired, it must, like the Eternal Spirit who guided its writers, be altogether true. And this line of reasoning has lately been powerfully vindicated by the findings of archaeology. By means of this science the supernatural accuracy of the Bible has been overwhelmingly demonstrated in recent times. As James Orr puts it, before the advent of archaeology

> Comparatively few materials existed, outside the Bible itself, for testing the correctness of the statements of that book regarding the peoples, countries, and civilizations, with which its pages, in so many different ways, bring us into contact. What information about ancient countries was derived from outside sources—as, e.g., from the Greek historian Herodotus —was late, confused, contradicted the Bible as well as confirmed it, and, of course, was freely used by unbelievers to discredit the authority of the Bible. By a singular providence of God, the state of things is very different now. Sixty years ago we were in the dark; now we are comparatively in a blaze of light. As if by magic, Egypt, Babylonia, Assyria, other ancient lands, have yielded up their buried palaces, their monuments, their long-lost libraries, a voice has gone up rebuking the scorner, and bearing a testimony, as emphatic as it was unlooked for, to the credibility of Holy Writ.
>
> — *The Bible Under Trial*

For instance, because of archaeological findings, no skeptic can ever again sneer at the account of the conquest of Jericho by the Israelites. Previously, mocking unbelievers took keen delight in pointing out the amusing absurdity of this narrative related in Scripture.

And the Lord said unto Joshua, See, I have given into thine hand Jericho, and the king thereof, and the mighty men of valour. And ye shall compass the city, all ye men of war, and go round about the city once. Thus shalt thou do six days. And seven priests shall bear before the ark seven trumpets of rams' horns: and the seventh day ye shall compass the city seven times, and the priests shall blow with the trumpets. And it shall come to pass, that when they make a long blast with the ram's horn, and when ye hear the sound of the trumpet, all the people shall shout with a great shout; and the wall of the city shall fall down flat, and the people shall ascend up every man straight before him. . . . And Joshua rose early in the morning, and the priests took up the ark of the Lord. And seven priests bearing seven trumpets of rams' horns before the ark of the Lord went on continually, and blew with the trumpets: and the armed men went before him; but the rereward came after the ark of the Lord, the priests going on, and blowing with the trumpets. And the second day they compassed the city once, and returned into the camp; so they did six days. And it came to pass on the seventh day, that they rose early about the dawning of the day and compassed the city after the same manner seven times: only on that day they compassed the city seven times. And it came to pass at the seventh time, when the priests blew with the trumpets, Joshua said unto the people, Shout; for the Lord hath given you the city. . . . So the people shouted when the priests blew with the trumpets: and it came to pass, when the people heard the sound of the trumpet, and the people shouted with a great shout, that the wall fell down flat, so that the people went up into the city, every man straight before him, and they took the city.

Joshua 6:2-20

What sport the skeptic once had with this story! The outstanding archaeologist, Professor John Garstang, who did not have the least concern about proving the truth of the Bible, carried on prolonged research at the site and discovered that, exactly as the Bible says, the city was thoroughly burned and destroyed while in occupation; and he also discovered that, exactly as the Bible says, the walls, somehow collapsing of their own accord, fell outwards, even though they were fifteen feet high and ten feet thick. In his own words: "There remains no doubt that the walls fell outwards so completely that the attackers would be able to clamber up and over their ruins into the city."

Archaeology has likewise demonstrated the literal truth of another narrative in the Bible which formerly was the butt of much skeptical irony — the destruction of Sodom and Gomorrah by a deluge of fire and brimstone, in the course of which the wife of Lot was encased in salt. Dr. A. Rendle Short, British surgeon, says:

> The Dead Sea has no outlet. The Jordan and other streams that flow into it bring down water and dissolved mineral salts; the water evaporates from the surface, and the salts become so concentrated that they are deposited in crystalline form in and around the lake. There is a stratum of rock salt 150 feet thick which can be traced for six miles. Overlying it is a layer of sulphur which can be lit with a match. Large quantities of bitumen (asphalt) used to exist around the lake; much has been taken away, but some remains. There is enough oil to cause an oil company, just before the Great War, to commence operations. The "slime pits" of Genesis XIV no doubt refer to the excavations for asphalt. It will be observed that the whole area is highly peculiar. If by

some act of God the gases generated in such a region became ignited, it is not at all surprising that fire and brimstone were rained upon Sodom and Gomorrah, that masses of salt hurled into the air may have covered over Lot's wife (the English translation that "She became a pillar of salt" gives a misleading sense), and that the smoke of the country went up as the smoke of a furnace. Kyle says a rupture of the strata is plainly visible. According to Alexis Mallon (1929), the site of Sodom shows that it was destroyed by a great fire, and never again occupied. Let us say in passing that we are not all disposed to explain away a miracle. It was by an act of God that Lot was warned and enabled to escape, and that the catastrophe occurred as it did and when it did.

If however, you are still inclined to doubt the literal truth of the Bible at this point, I suggest that you ponder a statement made by Commander Joseph B. Lynch of the United States Navy after he and a party of experts had carefully investigated the region of these cities. Here is his statement:

> It is for the learned to comment on the facts which we have laboriously collected. Upon ourselves, the result is a decided one. We entered upon this sea, with conflicting opinions. One of the party was skeptical, and another, I think, a professed unbeliever of the Mosaic account. After twenty-two days' close investigation, if I am not mistaken, we were unanimous in the conviction of the truth of the Scriptural account of the destruction of the cities of the plain.

So overwhelmingly has archaeology demonstrated the amazing accuracy of Scripture that several noted scholars who started out in skepticism and doubt became convinced believers, forced by sheer weight of fact to accept the Bible as the Word of the living God. I think of Dr. A. H. Sayce of England whom Prime Minister Gladstone refused to apppoint (in 1882) as professor of history at Oxford University because of the radical way in which he criticized the Bible. Then Sayce went to the Far East and personally began to dig up Biblical ruins, and as he did so he gradually became convinced that the Bible was right and he was wrong. And at last in 1898 he said that he had come to be regarded — and I give you his own words — "as a representative of the Orthodox Party and a defender of Holy Writ." I think, too, of Sir William Ramsay, famous authority on the ancient world. In his important book, *The Bearing of Recent Discovery on the Trustworthiness of the New Testament,* he tells how as a young professor he went to Palestine in order to study its antiquities for himself. At that time he did not accept the Bible as reliable history. He was especially persuaded that the Book of Acts in the New Testament was valueless as a factual record. He says, for instance, "At this point we are describing what reasons and arguments changed the mind of one who began under the impression that the history was written long after the events and that it was untrustworthy as a whole." Studying the findings of archaeology for himself he, like Dr. Sayce, became convinced that the Bible was right and he was wrong. He became so convinced of the Bible's accuracy that he finally declared to the whole world of modern scholarship, "I take the view that Luke's history is unsurpassed in regard to its trustworthiness . . . you may press the words of Luke in a degree beyond any other historian's and they stand the keenest scrutiny and the hardest treatment." Sir William Ramsay accepted the Bible as the Word of the Living God, and dedicated all his brilliant talents to the service of the redeeming Christ whom the Bible proclaims.

Science and Scripture

(I)

THE DISTINGUISHED AMERICAN PREACHER, Dr. Harry Emerson Fosdick, speaks in this critical and belittling fashion concerning the teachings of the Bible with respect to nature and science:

> When one moves back to the Scripture with a mind accustomed to work in modern ways, he finds himself in a strange world. . . . Knowing modern astronomy he turns to the Bible to find the sun and moon standing still or the shadow retreating on Ahaz' dial. Knowing modern biology he hears that when Elisha had been so long dead that only his bones were left, another dead body, thrown into the cave where he was buried, touched his skeleton and sprang to life again, or that after our Lord's resurrection many of the saints long deceased arose and appeared in Jerusalem. Knowing modern physics he turns to the Bible to read that light was created three days before the sun and that an axe-head floated when Elisha threw a stick into the water. Knowing modern medicine he finds in the Scripture many familiar ailments, epilepsy, deafness, dumbness, blindness, insan-

ity, ascribed to the visitation of demons. Knowing that the sky is blue because of the infinite number of dust particles that catch and break up the light, he finds himself in the Bible living under a solid "firmament" "strong as a molten mirror," or a "paved work of sapphire stone" from which a fiery chariot can come down to snatch a living man by literal levitation from the flat earth to his heavenly reward.

. . . .

We live in a new world. We have not kept the forms of thought and categories of explanation in astronomy, geology, biology, which the Bible contains. We have definitely and irrevocably gotten new ones diverse from and irreconcilable with the outlooks on the universe which earlier ages in general and the Bible in particular had.

Does the Bible abound with mistakes and inaccuracies of this kind? Does it contradict the established facts of astronomy, biology, chemistry, and physics? Is it scientifically untrustworthy? Not in the opinion of James Dwight Dana of Yale University, probably the most eminent geologist America has yet produced. He once addressed a graduating class in these words:

Young men! As you go out into the world to face scientific problems, remember that I, an old man who has known only science all his life long, say to you, that there is nothing truer in all the Universe than the scientific statements contained in the Word of God.

Is the Bible scientifically untrustworthy? Not in the opinion of Dr. Howard A. Kelly, of Johns Hopkins University, Baltimore. An authority on radium and herpetology and, in addition, a world-famous surgeon and gynecologist, he was a convinced and outspoken Christian, and included among his writings is that classic of common sense and spirituality, *A Scientific Man and the Bible*.

> A definite Christian faith is the one really important thing in life. I mean that literally. It is vastly more important than any profession; than any scientific research; than any other or all activities of a man's life. . . . My intimate experience has shown me that the Bible is a Living Word, just as definitely God's Word to me—and to every man who reads it—as a letter received in the morning's mail from my mother is her word to me. As such the Bible is its own defense and needs no apologist.
>
> — *American Magazine*

Is the Bible scientifically untrustworthy? Not in the opinion of Sir Ambrose Fleming who has been President of the Victoria Institute and Philosophical Society of Great Britain; President of the Television Society; Professor of Electrical Engineering in the University of London, Honorary Fellow of St. John's College and Cambridge Fellow of University College, London.

> Although there are a considerable number of educated persons in the leading nations of mankind who regard the remarkable Hebrew and Jewish literature called the Bible merely as the production of the unassisted human intellect embodying myths, legends, and the imaginations of men in unscientific ages rather than as in any way a supernatural revelation of truth, yet the fact remains that this literary masterpiece still retains, in spite of all attacks on it, a dominating position amongst human literature, and is an encyclopedic work which in extent of production, sale, world-wide circulation, and perusal is unapproached

by any other book or books ever written by mankind. It has a power of appeal to, and influence on, the learned and unlearned, powerful or simple, rich and poor, strong and feeble, civilized and uncivilized, possessed by no other set of books produced in the history of the world.

It has had to fight battles for existence against the most violent attempts to exterminate it, the like of which has been endured by no other book. Yet today it has been translated into every language spoken on earth, and printed and sold in numbers reckoned only in millions of copies. Whilst it is reverenced, loved, and treated by millions of those who have studied it as a supernatural book and in some way difficult to define, as a communication from the Creator of the Universe to Mankind, yet here again the greatest learning, cleverness, and ingenuity has been brought to bear upon it to undermine any belief of the above kind and represent it as the outcome of the human mind alone, having in it mistakes, inconsistencies, and fabrications, characteristic of imperfect human knowledge of events and facts.

Side by side with these attempts to minimize its value and distort its meaning or deny the truth of its history, there has been of late years an enormous increase in the discovery of facts which confirm its historical accuracy by the work of much archaeological research and exploration.

— *The Origin of Mankind*

Is the Bible scientifically untrustworthy? Not in the opinion of W. Bell Dawson, Gold Medalist in Geology and Natural Science at McGill University, and Laureate of the Academy of Science at Paris.

To the present writer, the Bible is a revelation from God of these higher truths, and of salvation through Christ. From a life-long study of the Scriptures, he is also convinced that in every subject which they touch upon, their every word is reliable, and deserves consideration; and this can only mean that they were written under Divine supervision and guidance.

If we will let the Bible speak for itself, we will be in a position to compare it with modern knowledge with some hope of enlightenment. We may thus find in the end, that the portrayal of nature and of man as set before us in the Scriptures, is not only corroborated by all that is most reliable in science; but that by accepting what the Bible states, we will invariably be pointed to the right road, and kept from the paths of error which would lead us astray in our advance in knowledge.

It is not, therefore, remarkable that the Bible, instead of looking to science for its confirmation, in reality anticipates the highest and deepest that science can reach; and not only so, but brings these within the limits of our comprehension. Surely, these are marks of Divine guidance and oversight; and they are reassuring to our belief that the Scriptures are a revelation from God.

Now why do you suppose these men of international repute look upon the Bible with profound respect and veneration? The reason for their attitude is this: not a single scientific inaccuracy in its pages has as yet been demonstrated. To be sure, many errors have been alleged, but it is one thing to allege a mistake and altogether another thing to prove that allegation. And the fact is that to date no error has been demonstrated. Do you know, for instance, that for years the Science Research Bureau, headed by the late Dr. Harry Rimmer, publicly offered a reward of one thousand dollars to any person who could prove the existence of a scientific blunder in the Bible? Although that offer has been made in twenty-seven different countries, the thousand dollars is still uncollected. But before you attempt to collect the reward, we ought to tell you that in November of 1939, William Floyd of New York City, thinking he had pointed out several bona fide inaccuracies, brought suit against Dr. Rimmer. The case was tried in the Fourth District Municipal Court with the Honorable Benjamin Shalleck on the bench. Mr. Floyd called in his own self-chosen witnesses to prove that the Bible from a scientific standpoint is fallacious. He lost the suit, and Justice Shalleck threw the case out of Court.

This absence of error in an ancient Book is truly remarkable, for all other ancient books, and even many recent ones, contain scientific blunders and mistakes. In the sacred writings of the Hindus, you find such fantastic nonsense as this: "The moon is 50,000 leagues higher than the sun and shines by its own light; night is caused by the sun's setting behind a huge mountain several thousand feet high, located in the center of the earth; this world, flat and triangular is composed of seven stages—one of honey, another of sugar, a third of butter, and still another of wine, and the whole mass is borne on the heads of countless elephants which in shaking produce earthquakes." Why is it that ridiculous teachings like these are nowhere to be discovered in the Bible, which is much more ancient than the sacred Vedas of India? Read the Koran and you find that the stars are torches set in the lower heavens, and that men are made out of baked clay! Or read the *Natural History* of Pliny, the Roman scientist who lived during the first century, and you are amused to note that he writes with equal satisfaction about "the lion, the unicorn, and the phoenix," unable to distinguish between the real and the imaginary, the true and the impossible. He perserves for us the superstition of the time and recounts in all good faith the practice of various forms of magic.

Why is it that the Bible, much older than the Vedas, or the Koran, or Pliny's *Natural History,* is not filled with the mistakes which are discoverable in their pages? Very plainly there is but one adequate explanation: a higher Intelligence than that of man has presided over the composition of the Bible and preserved its writers from error.

> Tested by cosmogony, astronomy, geology and zoology, physiology and comparative anatomy, natural philosophy and sanitary science, etc., this Book evinces superhuman knowledge and wisdom. It is a scientific marvel.
>
> — Dr. A. T. Pierson

But what does all this mean to us personally? Let a famous surgeon, Dr. D. M. Blair, Professor of Anatomy in the University of Glasgow, tell us what it ought to mean:

> The doctor who looks at the Bible finds himself in the end face to face with One who is greater than the Bible, greater than anyone he ever met; a Physician, the Great Physician, who can not only say to the stricken one, "Take up thy bed and walk," but also "Son, be of good cheer, thy *sins* are forgiven thee." Here is a matchless One, who can heal broken bodies, but also the souls of men.

"Those that are broken in their hearts and grieved in their minds, He healeth, and their painful wounds He tenderly upbinds."

The doctor looks back again along the way he has come. He has seen many things which he has recognized as true things, but now he sees a greater truth behind them all, One who *is* the Truth, of whom even Moses and the Prophets spake, when they "saw his glory and spake of him."

— *A Doctor Looks at the Bible* (1936)

Science and Scripture
(II)

DR. GEORGE WASHINGTON CARVER of Tuskegee, Alabama, was undoubtedly the greatest Negro scientist who has ever lived. It has been estimated that more than three freight cars would be required to carry samples of his many different discoveries, including some 300 from peanuts, nearly 200 from sweet potatoes, about 100 from pecans, and a large number from cotton, to say nothing of the synthetic products which he created out of waste materials. But Dr. Carver was not only a great scientist; he was also a great Christian. Once, when appearing before a Committee of the United States Senate to explain his experiments with the peanut, he was asked, "How did you learn all these things?" "From an old Book," he replied. "What book?" the Chairman inquired curiously. "The Bible," was Dr. Carver's answer. Indeed, that ancient Book was to him, as he frequently testified, an unfailing source of spiritual and scientific inspiration alike.

If a contemporary scientist were to sketch the stages by which our earth came to be as it now is, he would explain that originally there was only a watery mass and that out of this swirling sea the continents gradually emerged and were clothed with grass and trees, after which fish came into existence, then birds, next animals, and finally men. And, surprisingly enough, the Book of Genesis gives precisely the same sketch.

> Modern science may supplement, it is astonishing how little it requires us to reverse of, the ideas we derive from this narrative of the succession of steps in creation. . . . The dark watery waste over which the Spirit broods with vivifying power, the advent of light, the formation of an atmosphere or sky capable of sustaining the clouds above it, the settling of the great outlines of the continents and seas, the clothing of the dry land with abundant vegetation, the adjustment of the earth's relation to sun and moon as the visible rulers of its day and night, the production of the great sea monsters and reptile-like creatures (for these may well be included in "sheratzim") and birds, the peopling of the earth with four-footed beasts and cattle—last of all, the advent of Man—is there so much of all this which science requires us to cancel?
>
> — James Orr

Back in 1885 the noted prime minister of Great Britain, William Gladstone, who was a staunch believer in the full trustworthiness of the Bible, published a series of articles on the accuracy of Genesis which was attacked by Professor Thomas Huxley, the most brilliant scientist of that day. Gladstone suggested that they refer their debate to a distinguished American scientist and let him be the judge. "There is no one," Mr Huxley answered, "to whose authority I am more readily disposed to bow than that of my eminent friend Professor Dana." And the decision of Professor James Dwight Dana was this: "I agree in all essential points with Mr. Gladstone, and I believe that the first chapter of Genesis and science are in accord."

Nor was that the end of it. Six years later Sir Robert Anderson, the head of Scotland Yard, challenged Mr. Huxley on the same subject and the challenge was refused. So, as Sir Robert Anderson says in his book, *A Doubter's Doubts About Science and Religion*:

> The fact remains that Mr. Gladstone's position stands unshaken. The fact remains that one who has had no equal in this age as a scientific controversialist entered the lists to attack it, and retired discomfited and discredited. Mr. Gladstone's thesis, therefore, holds the field. "The order of creation as recorded in Genesis has been so affirmed in our time by natural science that it may be taken as a demonstrated conclusion and established fact." Are we then to conclude that when Genesis was written biological science was as enlightened and as far advanced as it is today? Or shall we adopt the more reasonable alternative, that "the Mosaic narrative" is a Divine revelation?

Modern physicists and astronomers have come to the conclusion that the heavens above and around us are an infinite expanse without any boundaries. A few centuries ago scientists held that the universe had definite limits and its measurements could be carefully figured out. Entirely in harmony with twentieth-century scientists, the Bible affirms that the heavens are an infinite expanse of space which cannot possibly be measured.

Thus saith the Lord; if heaven above can be measured, and the foundations of the earth searched out beneath, I will also cast off all the seed of Israel for all that they have done, saith the Lord.

—Jeremiah 31:7

For as the heavens are higher than the earth, so are my ways higher than your ways, and my thoughts than your thoughts.

—Isaiah 55:9

The infinite height of the heaven above the earth becomes the symbol of the infinite wisdom.

Once more in Psalms we read:

As far as the east is from the west, so far hath he removed our transgressions from us.

—Psalm 103:12

As Dr. A. T. Pierson comments:

The writer of the 103rd Psalm himself had no conception of what is known by us — that go as far as you will to the east there is still an east, and as far as you will go west, there is still a west; but God who spoke through him knew that only when you can measure the distance between the remotest east and west you can measure how far away from the forgiven sinner God has removed his sins — astronomical infinities are brought in to illustrate the infinity of the love and grace of God! There is no accident about that! It is manifestly intelligent design.

The invention of the telescope proved conclusively, as Sir James Jeans has put it, that, "It is no good trying to count the stars." Yet the astrologers of old thought that with patience and diligence such a census could be taken. In fact, they did count all the stars they were able to see, with the result that Hipparchus tallied 1022 and Ptolemy 1026. But the writers of the Bible, minus a telescope, were no less sure than Sir James Jeans with his telescope that "It is no good trying to count the stars."

> As the host of heaven cannot be numbered, neither the sand of the sea measured: so will I multiply the seed of David my servant, and the Levites that minister unto me.
>
> *Jeremiah 33:22*

And what is the promise which God made to Abraham?

> And he brought him forth abroad, and said, Look now toward heaven, and tell the stars, if thou be able to number them: and he said unto him, So shall thy seed be.
>
> *Genesis 15:5*

> And I will make thy seed as the dust of the earth, so that if a man can number the dust of the earth, then shall thy seed also be numbered.
>
> *Genesis 13:16*

Can anybody number the particles of dust in the world? No more can we number the twinkling lights in the sky above.

The surprising grasp of scientific truth such as the Bible writers had, led E. W. Maunder in his book, *The Astronomy of the Bible,* to declare that "by no process of research could man find for himself facts that are stated here. They must have been revealed."

In the Book of Job this rather casual challenge is flung out.

> Canst thou bind the sweet influences of Pleiades?
> *Job 38:31a*

On the surface that seems to be a bit of poetry and nothing more. But in actuality it has amazing implications. No wonder Sidney Collett writes:

> Pleiades is the name given by the ancient Greeks to what is known as "the seven stars." It comes from the Greek word *Pleein*—"to sail," and the appearance of this group indicated a favourable time for sailors to start on their voyage; it is also supposed to usher in the spring. But apparently little beyond this was known until recent years.
>
> The original Chaldaic word translated "Pleiades" is *Chimah* and means hinge or pivot, and the astronomer Bradley, in 1748, and more recently M. Madler of Dorpat and others, discovered, after much elaborate calculations, that Alcyone, the brightest of these seven stars, is actually, so far as is known, the center of our whole solar system — the hinge or pivot around which our sun, with all its attendant planets, is believed to revolve. Now when we remember that the sun is more than three thousand billion miles away from Alcyone, we get some idea of how marvellous must be the "influence" of the Pleiades, which swings these planets — the earth included — around it at the rate of more than one hundred and fifty million miles a year, in an orbit so vast that one circuit would occupy thousands of years to complete.
>
> Who can contemplate without an overwhelming sense of solemn awe the mighty power of God re-

ferred to in this remote verse in what is probably one of the oldest books in the Bible, and which recent astronomical discoveries enable us but dimly to appreciate?

As the ages roll on the heavenly bodies are ever in motion — the moon revolving around the earth; the earth with other planets revolving around the sun; the sun with all the solar system revolving around Alcyone: Alcyone with its myriad attendants revolving around some other unknown center; all these, and countless other creations, all unknown to man, revolving in awful grandeur around the center of all centers —the throne of the Almighty.

Moreover, it is worthy of notice that this "influence" is said to be "sweet," a word which in this connection is full of significance, as we think that our vast solar system with all its untold myriads of stars is ever moving at such an amazing pace, like some complex and mighty machinery, yet with a regularity and evenness that can only be described as "sweet"— the very word which engineers use today to describe perfectly smooth working.

— The Scripture of Truth

God's World-Transforming Word

I N THE COURSE of his four years at St. John's College, Annapolis, Maryland, every student is required to read nearly two hundred books ranging from ancient classics such as Homer's *Odyssey* to recent writings like those of Karl Marx and Sigmund Freud. The student becomes acquainted with those books which have exerted the most powerful and abiding influence upon the world.

Ernst Haeckel, the noted German scientist who was an untiring protagonist of atheistic rationalism, admitted the world-transforming power of the Bible when he said:

> Beyond all doubt the present degree of human culture owes, in great part, its perfection to the propagation of the Christian system of morals and its ennobling influence.

And George Romanes, the British physicist, made this somewhat similar statement:

> It is on all sides worth considering (blatant ignorance or base vulgarity alone excepted) that the revolution effected by Christianity in human life is immeasurable and unparalleled by any other movement in history.

But not only is Christianity thus so immeasurably in advance of all other religions. It is no less so of every other system of thought that has ever been promulgated in regard to all that is moral and spiritual. Whether it be true or false, it is certain that neither philosophy, science, nor poetry has ever produced results in thought, conduct, or beauty in any degree to be compared with it.

Only to a man wholly destitute of spiritual perception can it be that Christianity should fail to appear the greatest exhibition of the beautiful, the sublime, and of all else that appeals to our spiritual nature, which has ever been known upon our earth.

To see the world-transforming power of the Bible, consider the history of England.

England became the people of a book, and that book was the Bible. It was, as yet, the one English book which was familiar to every Englishman. It was read in churches, it was read at home, and everywhere its words, as they fell on ears which custom had not deadened to their force and beauty, kindled a startling enthusiasm. . . . Elizabeth might silence or tune the pulpits, but it was impossible for her to silence or tune the great preachers of justice and mercy and truth, who spoke from the book which the Lord again opened to the people. . . . The effect of the Bible in this way was simply amazing. The whole temper of the nation was changed. A new conception of life and of man superseded the old. A new moral and religious impulse spread through every class. . . . Theology rules there, said Grotius of England, only ten years after Elizabeth's death. The whole nation, in fact, becomes a church.

— J. H. Green,
Short History of the English People

Or listen to Hilaire Belloc, the distinguished Roman Catholic historian:

> England is and has long been fundamentally Protestant. Indeed no large proportion (i.e., of Englishmen) read the Bible habitually. But the mass of English agnostics and atheists are, in morals and outlook, of the same Bible-Christian kind as were their fathers.
>
> The whole body of English literature is Protestant.
>
> The Bible is everywhere woven into the stuff of the British.
>
> The astounding strength of Biblical influence on England, the depth to which it has penetrated the English mind, the universality of its effect and the extraordinary persistence of it in our own generation, when all the old religious basis of it is disappearing, proceeding from a special factor which only those to whom the English language is native can understand. This factor was the power of the Word.

Then, consider the remark of Goethe, the man-of-letters:

> Germany owes her freedom and her greatness to the open Bible, which Martin Luther found in the monastery at Erfurth and gave to the people in their own language. All the power of the German language, all its greatest men, and all its imperial progress, date from the time the German people were placed in possession of the Word of God in the common language.

Or turn from Germany to the United States, the stronghold of democracy. What is the foundation and source of American's greatness? The Bible!

A friend of Rufus Choate in looking over the large library of that outstanding lawyer remarked banteringly, "Seven editions of the New Testament and not a copy of the constitution!" To which Choate replied, "Ah, my friend, you forget that the constitution of my country is in them all."

And if you imagine that Rufus Choate was exaggerating, think about this: What is the origin of Lincoln's imperishable phrase, "Government of the people, by the people and for the people"? That phrase, which is the essence of democracy, comes from the introduction to Wycliffe's Bible, the first English Version of Holy Scripture. Here is the preface to that pioneer translation:

> The Bible will make possible a Government of people, by people, and for people.

James Russell Lowell, a noted writer with no particular affection for traditional Christianity, tells us:

> I fear that when we indulge ourselves in the amusement of going without a religion, we are not, perhaps, aware how much we are sustained by an enormous mass of religious feeling and religious conviction, so that, whatever it may be safe for us to think, for us who have had great advantages, and have been brought up in such a way that a certain moral direction has been given to our character, I do not know what would become of the less favoured classes of mankind, if they undertook to play the same game.

Then, after remarking that in his opinion Christianity certainly has some lamentable defects, he goes on to say that it is nevertheless

Infinitely preferable to any form of polite and polished skepticism, which gathers as its votaries the degenerate sons of heroic ancestors, who, having been trained in a society and educated in schools, the foundations of which were laid by men of faith and piety, now turn and kick down the ladder by which they have climbed up, and persuade men to live without God and leave them to die without hope. These men, indulging themselves in the amusement of going without a religion, may be thankful that they live in lands where the Gospel they neglect has tamed the beastliness and ferocity of the men who, but for Christianity, might long ago have eaten their carcasses like the South Sea Islanders, or cut off their heads and tanned their hides like the monsters of the French Revolution.

And Lowell concludes by suggesting that when the keen scrutiny of skeptics

Has found a place on this planet, ten miles square, where a decent man can live in decency, comfort, and security, supporting and educating his children unspoiled and unpolluted, a place where age is reverenced, infancy respected, womanhood honoured, and human life held in due regard, on this globe, where the Gospel of Christ has not gone and cleared the way and laid the foundations, and made decency and security possible, it will then be in order for the skeptical *literati* to move thither, and then ventilate their views. But so long as these men are very dependent on the religion which they discard for every privilege they enjoy, they may well hesitate a little before they seek to rob a Christian of his hope and humanity of its faith in that Saviour who alone has given to men that hope of eternal life which makes life tolerable and society possible, and robs death of its terrors and the grave of its gloom.

By way of additional illustration, consider what the Bible has done to advance the position of womankind. This is a crucial touchstone of a nation's real greatness, for as John Adams, the second president of the United States put it, the position of woman is "the most infallible barometer to ascertain the degree of morality in a nation." To learn what the Bible has achieved in this regard, we need not go back to Greece and Rome where the position of woman was degraded and her lot unenviable in the days before Christianity; all we need do is look at Japan where Christianity has hardly done more than scratch the surface. One observer declares:

> The daughter of the Japanese family has at the age of twenty but little development of her higher nature, very little indeed of the uplifting of the soul into the atmosphere above the routine of daily life. On the other hand, her master, man, pushing the principles of feminine obedience to the serving of his own selfishness, crushes out by trampling upon the most noble of feminine instincts. To satisfy his own needs, he degrades the glorious principle of feminine obedience into the depths of damnable abomination. A father in debt, an ambitious brother to get an education in order to win office, will sell the body of daughter or sister, even as the beasts are sold. Horribly significant is the proverb — "A father with many daughters need not fear poverty in old age."

Christianity does these six things which have elevated woman's position:

1.—Christianity teaches the spiritual equality of both sexes.
2.—Christianity insists that purity is as much incumbent upon men as women.
3.—Christianity maintains that marriage is a sacred and permanently binding contract.
4.—Christianity fights the current evil of easy divorce.
5.—Christianity improves the legal status of women.
6.—Christianity enlists in its service large numbers of the noblest women, to whom it gives unique opportunities for exercising those virtues which supremely characterize their sex.

Truly, as Caleb Cushing wrote:

The Christian religion levels upward, elevating all men to the same high standard of sanctity, faith and spiritual promise on earth as in heaven. Just so is it, that, wherever Christianity is taught, it inevitably dignifies and exalts the female character.

The Bible possesses a world-transforming power because it possesses a life-transforming power. The Bible is able to change nations and customs only because, to begin with, it is able to change the hearts and characters of men. Probably there is no more sensational example of the life-transforming power of the Bible than the unbelievable story of *Mutiny on the Bounty*. In 1887 the Bounty, under Captain Bligh, set sail for the island of Tahiti in the South Seas. After a voyage of ten months, the ship arrived at her destination, and further six months were spent collecting palm saplings. The sailors meanwhile had become attached to the native girls, so upon receiving the order to embark, they mutinied, set the captain and a few men adrift in an open boat, and returned to the island.

Captain Bligh, however, survived his ordeal and eventually arrived home in England. A punitive expedition was sent out, which captured fourteen of the mutineers. But nine of them had transferred to another island, where they formed a new colony. Here, in the language of the Encyclopedia Britannica, they degenerated so fast and became so fierce as to make the life of the colony a hell on earth. The chief reason for this was the distillation of whiskey from a native plant. Quarrels, orgies and murders were a common feature of their life. Finally all the men except one were killed or had died off. Alexander Smith was left alone with a crowd of native women and half-breed children. Then a strange thing happened. In a battered chest he found a Bible. He read it, believed it, and began to live it. Determining to make amends for his past evil life, he gathered the women and children around him and taught them too. Time rolled on. The children grew up and became Christians. The community prospered exceedingly. Nearly twenty years later an American ship visited the island and brought back to Europe and England word of its peaceful state. The British Government took no further action. There was no need. The island was a Christian community. There was no disease, no insanity, no crime, no illiteracy, and no strong drink. Life and property were safe, and the moral standards of the people were as high as anywhere in the world. It was a veritable Utopia on a small scale. What had brought about this astounding transformation? Just the reading of a book, and that book the Bible.

Think of the miracle which occurred in the life of Henry Moorhouse. Here is Richard Day's picturesque description of his career:

Born in Ardwich, in 1840, he was hell-bent-on-high by the time he was twenty; a cocky little bantam-weight prizefighter, battling equally vs. men and alcohol. At nineteen he was done for. One night, in an excess of remorse, he stood in a dark hall toying with a loaded pistol. Someone was holding a little meeting overhead, door open; he heard a voice reading the Prodigal Son, and the mystery of conviction covered his poor soul. Just the Word! And a few weeks later, a faithful fireman in a Manchester warehouse basement brought him to light with Romans 10:9-10. Just the Word!

He at once began to witness with *just the Word* in the mission rooms. No one "cared enough about the little runt" to suggest a course of study. So he kept to just the Word; soaked it up; flavored himself therewith to the fingertips. Within four years, he was a bright and shining light. Men from every strata, burly colliers or brainy courtiers, sat spellbound before him. In 1879 his health crumbled. Physicians told him, "You must stop — your heart!" "How long will I live if I stop?" "Probably eighteen months." "And if I keep on?" "Perhaps nine months." "Very well, I'll take the nine months, and preach Christ as long as I can." On December 25, 1880, he spent his first Christmas in heaven, after twenty years of incredibly fruitful ministry in the Word, intercessory prayer, and life changing.

The apostle Paul exclaims: "The word of God is quick and powerful." And this Book, the Word of God, which has been able to change nations is able to change your own life if you will but read it and believe it. For, in the words of Dr. R. S. Storr:

While the Bible has changed the face of Europe, building cathedrals, hospitals, universities, and has covered this country with at least the foundations and lower stories of its appropriate civilization, while it has made the enlightened and aspiring Christendom of today the fact of chief importance thus far in the progress of mankind — its true glory is that it has wiped the tears of sorrow from the eyes of its disciples, and has comforted hearts which were desolate with grief; that it has given celestial visions to those who dwelt beneath thatched roofs, and has taught a happier humility to the proud; that it has shed victorious tranquillity on those who have seen the shadows of death closing around them, and has caused to be written over their graves the lofty words of promise and cheer, "I am the Resurrection and the Life."

Redemption versus Religion

AS A RULE while there is much talking about religion, very little serious thinking is done in regard to it. And it is for that reason, perhaps, that so frequently you hear the remark, "Any religion is good enough, provided its followers are sincere." It is for that reason, too, no doubt, that on every hand it is simply taken for granted that a man's choice of religion is purely a matter of personal preference, like the kind of tie he wears or the style of hat he prefers; and, consequently, since religion is purely a matter of personal preference, it is the height of intolerance to find fault with a man's convictions on this point. Therefore, the only proper attitude to assume is that of broad-minded indifferentism toward beliefs which may conflict with your own. In her syndicated column, *My Day,* Mrs. Franklin D. Roosevelt, whose opinion commands attention and respect, recently said this:

> I keep getting letters which point up the prejudices in which so many of us indulge, even in wartime. They are not always prejudices against a race, sometimes they are religious prejudices. For instance, some people do not wish to be where Catholics or Jews predominate in their environment. Sometimes, it is Protestants who are banned.

All this seems out of place in a country with so many racial origins and so many religions. Our soldiers fight and die, side by side, and are comforted by priests, ministers, or rabbis, as the case may be, quite regardless of whether the dying boy belongs to the particular church represented near them at the moment.

It seems to me this might teach us, as civilians, a lesson. What is really important is not what religion or race we belong to, but how we live our lives, whether we deal with others with honesty and kindness, or whether we lie and cheat and take advantage of our neighbors. I wish that out of this war might come to us a truer evaluation of the worth of human beings and far less interest in the labels of race and religion.

To argue that any religion is good enough provided its followers are sincere is to make sincerity the final test of truth. But the ordinary experiences of life continually prove that a man may be sincerely wrong, and if so, all his sincerity does not avert pain and sorrow and disaster. A chemist may sincerely mix together the wrong ingredients and, despite his sincerity, blow himself and his laboratory into fragments. A salesman, hurrying to make connections, may sincerely take the wrong train and, despite his sincerity, arrive at a place miles away from his desired destination, and so lose out on a valuable contract. A mother, groping about for medicine at night in a dark room, may sincerely give her sick child a wrong prescription and, despite her sincerity, cause agony and even death. Unless a religion squares with the facts of history and human experience; and unless it agrees with the truth of God which is the underlying reality of all things, that religion. however sincere its followers may be, is not good enough. Truth, after all, is truth, whether in surgery, or mathematics, or science; no self-respecting mathematician tolerates mistakes in an algebraic problem. No self-respecting surgeon is broad-mindedly indifferent as to the right or wrong operational technique. No self-respecting scientist carelessly shrugs his shoulders and lets error go by unchallenged.

The opinion that any religion is good enough provided its followers are sincere is contrary to the teachings of the Bible. If the Bible is indeed the Word of God; if it is indeed a supernatural revelation of what the Creator of men desires them to know and believe and do; if it is indeed the only infallible guide for faith and practice; then of course the Bible is the Supreme Court in the sphere of religion. Then, of course, we must accept and abide by its decisions. Then all our own opinions must be brought into conformity with it. What, therefore, has God said concerning broad-minded indifferentism in religion? Does the Bible indiscriminately sanction all creeds as so many different highroads to a blessed eternity? Or does it dogmatically set forth one faith and one alone as the way to the glory of God and the God of glory?

> There is a way which seemeth right unto a man,
> but the end thereof are the ways of death.
>
> *Proverbs 14:12*

It is evident, then, that not every and any way which a man may choose to follow is of God's appointment and enjoys God's approval, even though the way seem right and be sincerely adhered to. Unless a man is walking in the right way, the end of his journey will be death, and death in Scripture is the symbol of exile from the glory of God and the God of glory.

> I am the way, the truth, and the life: no man cometh unto the Father, but by me.
>
> *John 14:6*

Listen also to these words of the Lord Jesus:

> I am the door: by me if any man enter in, he shall be saved, and shall go in and out, and find pasture.
>
> *John 10:9*

Or listen to the apostle Peter:

> Neither is there salvation in any other; for there is none other name under heaven given among men, whereby we must be saved.
>
> *Acts 4:12*

Listen likewise to the apostle Paul:

> For other foundation can no man lay than that is laid, which is Jesus Christ.
>
> *I Corinthians 3:11*

In that day when the floods of judgement thunder and the winds of judgment howl, all other foundations will give way. Only faith in the crucified Son of God will then avail.

Why do you suppose the Bible repeatedly urges, "Believe on the Lord Jesus Christ, and thou shalt be saved" (Acts 16:31)?

Why do you suppose it repeatedly asserts, "He that believeth on the Son hath everlasting life: and he that believeth not the Son shall not see life; but the wrath of God abideth on him" (John 3:36)?

The Bible does so because, whatever man may think, God does not look upon religion as a matter of indifference.

In His eyes there can be only one saving faith, and that is the faith made possible by His grace, the faith commanded in His Word, the faith which centers in the loving and atoning sacrifice of Jesus Christ.

The widespread opinion that any religion is good enough, provided its followers are sincere, is contrary to experience. Not every religion endows a man with peace that passeth all understanding. Only faith in Christ can do that. What other religion gives a man courage to face the hardest tests and trials of life with a song? What other religion brings into the heart of a man the joyous certainty that all his sins have been completely and forever forgiven? What other religion enables a man to walk through the valley of the shadow of death without fear and doubting? And certainly no other religion places at a man's disposal the infinite resources of God's omnipotence for battle against besetting temptations and inborn weaknesses. Only faith in Christ can do that.

A searching test of any religion is this: What are its fruits in human life? Does it produce love, joy, peace, long-suffering, goodness, gentleness, meekness and temperance? Whatever the various religions of the world may be able to do in bringing forth this fruit, faith in Jesus Christ most certainly has the power of generating all these qualities in the depths of men's hearts. Pierre Loti, the French literary genius, was not a Christian and can therefore be accepted as an unprejudiced witness. Here, then, is what he wrote concerning this:

> Those who still bow before the feet of Christ know nothing of the anguish of passing time, the anguish of loneliness and the terror of coming extinction. They go on their way confident and calm. I

would give my life to possess that radiant illusion of theirs, even at the risk of becoming as infatuated as the poor lunatics in asylums who fancy themselves among the rich and powerful of earth. In default of this faith could we but anchor ourselves to something, some hope, some immortality — but there is nothing. Outside of this ever-shining personality of Christ everything is terror and darkness.

From the Orient comes the story of a man who dreamed that he had stumbled into a deep pit where he lay in helpless despair. A Confucianist, passing by, leaned over the edge of the hole and shouted down, "Friend, let me give you some good advice. If you ever get out of your trouble, see to it that you never get into it again." Shortly afterwards a Buddhist passing by leaned over the edge of the hole and shouted down, "Friend, if you manage to climb up so that I can grab your hand, I will help you out." Then in the dream Christ passed by and, hearing the groans of despair, descended into the pit and climbed out with the man on His shoulders. That is the difference between mere religion and faith in the Lord Jesus. Religion may offer you sage advice and make an ineffectual effort to help you help yourself, but Christ, descending to the level of your wretchedness and impotence, lifts you up into liberty and joy. That was why when challenged by a Chinese statesman, "What right have you Christians to bring your gospel to this country where we have our own religions?" the missionary answered, "The right to give to others something too good to keep."

Are you experiencing love and joy and peace in your heart? If not, a different religion can offer you no help.

What you need is to enter by faith into a redeeming relationship with the Lord Jesus Christ.

Dr. W. Graham Scroggie, formerly pastor of Spurgeon's Tabernacle, London, published a book of excerpts from the diaries of his mother, a woman of extraordinary judgment and spiritual insight. This is one of her comments:

> The Gospel is God's power, and is enough for all His purpose. I know of nothing more urgent today than that men and women engaged in the recognized service of Christ should be soundly converted to God. Class-leaders, Sunday School Teachers, Organists, Members of Choirs, Secretaries, Treasurers, Elders, Deacons, and even Ministers of Churches, in numberless cases, have never stood behind the sheltering blood, have never been delivered from the guilt of sin, or come into possession of the life of God. Everybody finds it necessary to have so much religion, but religion does not save. Cain was one of the most devoted religionists who ever trod the soil. Once an old woman, asked if she had religion, replied, "No, thank God, I've lost that, it was nearly the death of me, and now I have Christ." I would to God that the multitude of our religionists today would make the same fruitful exchange.

Old Truths for New Times

WHAT IS THE ASSUMPTION underlying this statement by Clifford Kirkpatrick, who is one of the leaders of contemporary liberalism?

> It is amazing that primitive conceptions of the universe, developed some three thousand years ago in Arabia, are spoken with greater conviction than ever into a tiny microphone and sent winging their way into thousands of homes.

That indirect reference to Christianity assumes that simply because the gospel is antique it has no value for the twentieth century. That same assumption underlies this statement by Harry Elmer Barnes:

> In a truly scientific age a man would be as much humiliated and disgraced to defend the literal inspiration of the Bible . . . as he would be today if he were compelled to travel daily down Fifth Avenue, New York, in an ox-cart or to use stone implements in consuming his soup at a metropolitan banquet.

According to Dr. Barnes, the progress of knowledge compels mankind to scrap completely the religious heritage passed down through the ages before the invention of the telescope and microscope and airplane.

Now, to be sure, science has revolutionized the world; but although man's world has been changed, man himself is still what he always was and what he will be. As Goethe aptly expressed it, "Mankind is always changing but man is always the same." Kingdoms may topple and dictatorships arise; ox-carts may give place to airplanes; huts may evolve into skyscrapers with elevators; flickering candles may vanish in the blaze of electric lights; but regardless of all this, human nature with its wants and needs is still the same. The sophisticated New Yorker who zooms to his luxurious apartments on the twenty-second floor is essentially no different from the nomad who wandered over the plateaus of the Holy Land in the age of Abraham. The New Yorker and the nomad share the same emotions of fear and joy and sorrow; they have the same hopes and longings; they are beset by the same passions and lusts; they know the same hunger of heart. Is man in the twentieth century so different from what men used to be that he no longer does wrong and then confesses with burning shame as the Psalmist did?

> Wash me thoroughly from mine iniquity, and cleanse me from my sin. For I acknowledge my transgressions: and my sin is ever before me. Against thee, thee only have I sinned, and done this evil in thy sight.
>
> *Psalm 51:2-4*

The development of science has not changed our experience of sin and our anguish to be cleansed from its guilt.

Is man in the twentieth century so different from what men used to be that he no longer stands on the brink of a new grave and laments as David did?

> O my son Absalom, my son, my son Absalom!
> would God I had died for thee, O Absalom, my son,
> my son!
>
> *II Samuel 18:33b*

The invention of the telescope or microscope in no
way alters our experience of heartbreak in the hour of
death.

Is man in the twentieth century so different from what
men used to be that in the face of suffering and war and
life's major mysteries he no longer inquires as Gideon did

> Why then is all this befallen us?
>
> *Judges 6:13*

The erection of lofty buildings and the construction of
smoother highways cannot touch our experience of bewilderment as we ponder the why and wherefore of human
life.

Is man in the twentieth century so different from what
men used to be that he no longer knows the inner thrill
and ecstasy which flamed in the heart of Jacob, as Genesis
puts the story with exquisite simplicity:

> And Jacob served seven years for Rachel, and they
> seemed unto him but a few days, for the love he had
> to her.
>
> *Genesis 29:20*

Is man in the twentieth century so different from what
men used to be that he no longer hungers and thirsts
after God, crying with Job, "Oh that I knew where I might
find him!" or exclaiming with the Psalmist, "As the hart
panteth after the water brooks, so panteth my soul after
thee, O God"? Has the multiplication of conveniences and

comforts done anything at all to satisfy this hunger or slake this thirst?

Is man in the twentieth century so different that he no longer yearns for "joy unspeakable and full of glory"? Is he so different that he no longer desires "peace which passeth all understanding"? Is he so different that he no longer wants to have "full assurance" concerning the untraveled country beyond the doorway of death? Is twentieth-century man with all his impressive array of gadgets happy and contented? No, he is not; as author Will Durant writes:

> We move about the earth with unprecedented speed, but we do not know, and have not thought, where we are going, or whether we shall find any happiness there for our harassed souls. We are being destroyed by our knowledge, which has made us drunk with our power.

So, then, if man is essentially the same as he always has been, Christianity is not yet superfluous and meaningless. For man in his sin needs God's pardoning grace, and only the gospel can supply that. Man in his heartbreak needs a healing consolation, and only the gospel can supply that. Man in his bewilderment needs a satisfactory explanation of life's mysteries. In his hunger of heart he needs the fellowship and friendship of the everlasting God. If the good news of salvation through faith in Jesus Christ brought joy and peace and certainty to needy souls in all the days gone by, it can do so now in these chaotic days of the twentieth century. God has not changed. The gospel has not changed. Humanity has not changed. The old gospel will still do if men will but accept and believe it.

Long generations ago the Lord Jehovah reproached the Israelites because they foolishly fancied that a change of the circumstances around them necessitated a new religion. This was the burden of His complaint:

> Hath a nation changed their gods, which are yet no gods? but my people have changed their glory for that which doth not profit. . . . For my people have committed two evils; they have forsaken me the fountain of living waters, and hewed them out cisterns, broken cisterns, that can hold no water.
>
> *Jeremiah 2:11, 13*

The world today is copying the Israelites of old; it is turning away from the fountain of living water; it is abandoning the gospel of God's grace, simply because twentieth-century man has a phobia for anything old-fashioned and a mania for anything novel. The world, its soul burningly athirst, is frantically hewing out cisterns of philosophy, speculation and pseudo-religion. But alas, all of these are broken cisterns and hold no water. Not until the world returns to Jesus Christ, the fountain of living water, will its intolerable thirst at last be slaked.

I know, of course, that this can be dismissed as "putting the clock back." But listen to what C. S. Lewis of Oxford University has written on this score:

> Would you think I was joking if I said that you *can* put a clock back, and that if the clock is wrong it's often a very sensible thing to do? But I would rather get away from that whole idea of clocks. We all want progress. But progress means getting nearer to the place where you want to be. And if you've taken a wrong turning, then to go forward does *not* get you any nearer. If you're on the wrong road,

progress means doing an about-turn and walking back to the right road; and in that case the man who turns back soonest is the most progressive man. We've all seen this at our jobs, haven't we? When I have started a bit of work the wrong way, the sooner I admit this and go back and start over again, the faster I shall get on. There's nothing progressive about being pigheaded and refusing to admit a mistake. And I think if you look at the present state of the world, it's pretty plain that humanity has been making some big mistake. We're on the wrong road. And if that is so, we must go back. Going back is the quickest way on.

Yes, in our phobia for anything which might be out-of-date, we have been going wrong, dead wrong. And, therefore, we must turn back to the old-fashioned gospel, the gospel of atonement for sin by substitutionary sacrifice, the gospel of grace and glory, the gospel of judgment and justification, the gospel of Golgotha with its blood-stained cross and the Garden with its empty tomb. We must turn back to that gospel, for only in that gospel will the unchanging hunger of our souls be satisfied.

In this twentieth century you need God's old-fashioned salvation with its new joy, new peace, new hope, new power and new life; you can have it all through faith in Jesus Christ.

The Why of War

SOME YEARS AGO, during World War II, while glancing through a popular magazine, I came upon a page of pictures which horrified me. I stared at them incredulously. Was it possible that I was living in the twentieth century with its boasted culture and vaunted progress, or was I in the unenlightened ages when savage force was the court of last appeal? Those little children with their mangled bodies, why had they in their childish innocence been so brutally bombed? That hospital, far removed from the trenches, why had it been so cruelly demolished and the broken bodies within its walls broken further? And as I stared I thought of the unutterable carnage of which those photographs were but samples; and as I thought of that, and thought too of the limitless pity, the unbounded love of the heavenly Father, there rose within my soul the exclamation, "Oh, God, *why*?" Not an outburst of unbelief, but an expression of bewilderment in the face of the naked realities of life.

Now it is somewhat reassuring to learn that such an agonized inquiry has risen in the troubled hearts of devout men in centuries past; for there is really nothing new under the sun, and the calamities which overwhelm us are by no means a novelty in human history. Thus, for instance, we can turn to the ancient prophet Habakkuk and observe that he too was perplexed by devastating injustice and unrighteousness. His lot was cast, as ours is, in an era of confusion and chaos. He lived, in all probability, during the tumultuous days of wicked King Manasseh when the irresistible, terrifying armies of Chaldea were laying waste the nations of Asia. And Habakkuk could not understand why, despite his most fervid prayers, the heavens were sealed and Jehovah did not answer. His patience finally wore thin, and he well-nigh rebuked the Lord:

> How long shall I cry, and thou wilt not hear! even cry out unto thee of violence and thou wilt not save!
>
> *Habakkuk 1:2*

Puzzled and distressed, he subjected God to cross-examination:

> Why dost thou show me iniquity, and cause me to behold grievance? for spoiling and violence are before me: and there are that raise up strife and contention. Therefore the law is slacked, and judgment doth never go forth: for the wicked doth compass about the righteous; therefore wrong judgment proceedeth.
>
> *Habakkuk 1:3-4*

> Thou art of purer eyes than to behold evil, and canst not look on iniquity: wherefore lookest thou upon them that deal treacherously, and holdest thy

tongue when the wicked devoureth the man that is
more righteous than he?

Habakkuk 1:13

The Chaldean tyrant had outraged humanity; misery,
disorder, and wrong filled the earth as the waters cover the
sea, and God did nothing about it! Driven to his wit's end
by brutal facts, Habakkuk demanded *why*.

This is still a fundamental problem of thought, a
question which wells up continually now, and will not
subside because of World War II with its unspeakable
horrors, with its millions of soldiers and civilians who
have been wounded, blinded, crippled, raped, exiled,
maddened, butchered! O God, *why?* Why, O merciful
Father? How can divine love be harmonized with the
misery of human experience? How can it possibly be?
So grave is this difficulty which cannot honestly be ignored,
that the English philosopher, John Stuart Mill declared that
"the problem of reconciling infinite benevolence and justice
in the Creator of such a world as this" is insoluble. I
cannot agree with Mill, but I can appreciate his perplexity,
for as Edwin Booth once wrote to a friend of his, "Life
is a great big spelling book, and on every page we turn
the words grow harder to understand the meaning of."
Life is indeed like that; and everybody who thinks about
these things must confess that here is a problem whose
meaning we can scarcely understand.

Once more I would refer you to the Word of the Lord
as we have it in Habakkuk, the prophet who impatiently
and insistently asks, "Why?" After raising the problem in
its acutest form, the puzzled interrogator decides to "watch
to see what he will say to me, and what I shall answer when

I am reproved" (Hab. 2:1) And as he hopefully lingers, the voice of Jehovah answers:

> The vision is yet for an appointed time, but at the end it shall speak, and not lie; though it tarry, wait for it; because it will surely come, it will not tarry.
>
> *Habakkuk 2:3*

Now what is the essential meaning of this reply? God counsels the heavy-hearted, baffled Habakkuk, "Wait and see. A day is assuredly coming, as assuredly as I, Jehovah, live, in which injustice will be righted, evil will be fully and finally punished, and the tangled riddles of life happily unraveled. Trust in Me, and be patient. Rest upon the assurance that the Judge of all the earth will do right."

Here, then, is one case where we must take our faith down from the shelf and put it to work. Believing where we cannot clearly understand, trusting where we cannot see, we must affirm with Paul, "All things work together for good to them that love God" (Rom. 8:28). We must affirm, as did Alfred Lord Tennyson:

> O yet we trust that somehow good
> Will be the final goal of ill,
> To pangs of nature, sins of will,
> Defects of doubt and taints of blood —
> That nothing walks with aimless feet,
> That not one life will be destroyed,
> Or cast as rubbish to the void,
> When God hath made the pile complete.
> — *In Memoriam*

We must affirm, as does one of our favorite hymns:

> Not now, but in the coming years,
> It may be in that Better Land,
> We'll read the meaning of our tears,
> And there sometime we'll understand.
> We'll catch the broken threads again,
> And finish what we here began.
> Heaven will *all mysteries explain,*
> And there, up there, we'll understand.

Let us frankly recognize the limits of our minds. Let us realize that we now see in a glass darkly and know but partially and imperfectly. And if our faith in God is more than a meaningless verbal assent to His existence, let us leave the full explanation to Him to disclose in His own appointed time. And meanwhile, let us wait and trust!

In His own time God will give a satisfying solution to this troublesome enigma. "Shall not the Judge of all the earth do right?" To ask the question is to answer it.

But, in addition to this consideration, do not forget that the Bible everywhere teaches the solemn, little-liked truth that man himself, not God, is responsible for all human misery. Scripture emphatically announces that man is a sinner who has deliberately, of his own free will, revolted against the loving Creator. And the bitter fruit of sin is suffering and sorrow. Hence, as a willful transgressor, man lies under the judgment of God, a judgment, both remedial and retributive, which expresses itself at times in calamities like earthquakes, floods, and wars.

How replete the Old Testament is with instance after instance of this principle! Verily, one of its major teachings is that many a catastrophe is a divine visitation because of human depravity and disobedience. This is brought out plainly in the Book of Judges. With the Midianites ravaging the country of Israel, with the people of God undergoing terrible affliction, it seemed as if Jehovah had abdicated His throne. And thus Gideon, the chieftain of the Jews, almost angrily asked, "If the Lord be with us, why then is all this befallen us?" (Judges 6:13). And the explanation given through the Lord's unnamed prophet was simply: "Ye have not obeyed my voice" (Judges 6:10). The calamity of the Midianite invasion came as a divine visitation because of Israel's depravity and disobedience.

And what is the colossal disaster of the present war but terrible judgment because of terrible sin? God has been forgotten. His law has been brazenly broken. Deplorable licentiousness has reigned unchecked. The love of Heaven has been mockingly spurned. The bloody cross of Calvary, the supreme revelation of divine mercy, has been passed by, laughed at, spat upon! And the long-restrained judgment of outraged Deity is now being unleased upon a Bible-hating, Christ-rejecting civilization.

The principle of calamity as a divine visitation because of human disobedience is brought out also in the prophecy of Jeremiah. The Jews lamented as Nebuchadnezzar, with his mighty engines of destruction and his ingenious methods of torture, ransacked their towns, slaughtered the inhabitants and carried the remnant into a captivity that was a living death. They protested indignantly, "Lord, Thou art unjust. Why dost Thou permit these things?" And through Jeremiah, Jehovah spoke:

> Why criest thou for thine afflictions? thy sorrow
> is incurable for the multitude of thine iniquity:

because thy sins are increased, I have done these things
unto thee.

Jeremiah 30:15

The same principle is brought out again in the prophecy of Daniel. In a notable confession, made when
Israel was in exile, the prophet sadly states time and again,
"These calamities have come upon us because we have
knowingly sinned against God." The nations of the world
must make that same sorrowful confession, admitting with
Daniel, "The Lord is righteous in all his works which he
doeth."

Yes, God is indeed righteous in everything He per-
mits, even this horrible war. For humanity as a whole,
after nearly twenty centuries have ebbed away, continues,
increasingly so, to turn aside from the Lord and to trample
under foot the precious blood of Jesus Christ. Consequently,
judgment is falling. So as we raise our puzzled question,
"Why?" let us not forget that man, as the author of his
destiny, is alone responsible for the world's misery because
he continues to sin against God. And catastrophe will
doubtless come upon the heels of catastrophe until the
nations repent, forsake their evil ways, and cry aloud for
mercy that is never denied.

And let us not forget, furthermore, another reassuring
fact which is stated in the Psalms:

Surely the wrath of man shall praise thee: the
remainder of wrath shalt thou restrain.

Psalm 76:10

God does not create evil, but in His omnipotence He
utilizes the very injustice and unrighteousness of man to
work out His own program. However much we clamor

for Him to arrange affairs to please us, to terminate our misfortunes, to make wars to cease, sometimes He will ignore us, because we pray in ignorance not realizing that God is making the very wrath of man to praise Him.

Do not imagine, therefore, that this war is some uncalculated misfortune which upsets Heaven as well as earth. This calamity will be utilized by God in the outworking of His eternal purposes. The very wrath of man will yet praise Him.

And now, how do these things touch your life and mine? Are the facts which have been presented abstract, remote, too theoretical to help us as we face the brutal realities of the present war? Are they meaningful for each of us personally? It seems to me they are.

If we are Christians, let us have humility enough to confess that the complete solution is beyond us. Let us have faith enough to trust in God, believing that He can and some day will explain this enigma. Let us have courage enough to declare unflinchingly that war is the tragic, ugly consequence, not merely of economic maladjustments and racial differences, but ultimately of tragic, ugly sin, notably the sin of man's willful rejection of God's love in the cross of Christ. Let us, then, summon men to repentance, and let us give ourselves to fervent prayer as never before.

If you are not a Christian, realize that war is a divine visitation because of human disobedience. And as you realize that judgment is righteously devastating the world because of your sin, your neighbor's sin, and the sin of millions exactly like you, fall on your knees in contrition and confession, and cry aloud to God for mercy in the prevailing name of Jesus Christ, praying that all your guilt may be pardoned because of the blood sacrificially poured out upon Calvary. Oh, if you do that, and if multiplied others like you do it, the wrath of God will be restrained, and in the wake of spiritual revival, peace will come. And though war may continue to rage for some time, in your own heart will be the tranquillity which is the portion of only those who were rebels but are now reconciled to God through Christ.

The Wisdom of the World
(I)

THE MATERIALIST arrogantly asserts that there is no essential difference between a man and a dog, or a horse, or a gorilla. Regardless of his positiveness, however, the materialist is wrong. and he is wrong for three reasons. In the first place, man is different from animals because he alone possesses a spirit which gives him God-consciousness. In the second place, man alone possesses freedom of will. He can choose his own course of action, and no dog or horse or gorilla has the power to do that; it follows the prompting of its instincts. In the third place, man alone possesses the godly faculty of reason. Of course, I admit that a dog may have some sort of rudimentary intelligence, but between the intelligence of a dog and the intelligence of a man there is a measureless gulf. And I for one will believe that there is no essential difference between the intelligence of a dog and the intelligence of a man only when the materialist can show that a dog has written a textbook on mathematics or astronomy.

Man's reason is a precious gift of God upon which

we ought never to look with contempt. However Godlike
the human reason may be, when man through pride
sinfully perverts his mind, it is no longer worthy of respect.

> For the wrath of God is revealed from heaven
> against all ungodliness and unrighteousness of men,
> who hold the truth in unrighteousness; because that
> which may be known of God is manifest in them; for
> God hath showed it unto them. For the invisible
> things of him from the creation of the world are
> clearly seen, being understood by the things that are
> made, even his eternal power and Godhead; so that
> they are without excuse: because that, when they
> knew God, they glorified him not as God, neither
> were thankful; but became vain in their imaginations,
> and their foolish heart was darkened. Professing
> themselves to be wise, they became fools, and changed
> the glory of the uncorruptible God into an image
> made like to corruptible man, and to birds, and four-
> footed beasts, and creeping things.
>
> *Romans 1:18-23*

> And even as they did not like to retain God in
> their knowledge, God gave them over to a reprobate
> mind, to do those things which are not convenient.
>
> *Romans 1:28*

Consequently, human wisdom in its godless self-
sufficiency is frequently stupid, and, as Paul points out, the
sages and thinkers of this world, professing themselves to
be intellectually profound, are really pitifully silly.

The folly of human wisdom can be illustrated, I
think, in three ways. To begin with, turning away from
the knowledge of the true and living God, men become
fools because they embrace the philosophy of atheism. They

unintelligently deny the existence of their own Creator.
They do it, no doubt, in the name of science and scholar-
ship, and with an imposing display of logic and learning.
But what does the Psalmist say about them?

> The fool hath said in his heart, There is no God.
> *Psalm 53:1*

Yet how amazing it is that many outstanding thinkers
who profess to be extremely wise have in their foolishness
dared to deny God. Take, as an example, Karl Marx, the
godfather of modern Russia. It was he who sneered,
"Religion is the opiate of the people." It was he who taught
that faith in God and Jesus Christ must be wiped away
from the face of the earth because it is an impediment to
the progress of human society. It was he who insisted that
his followers be avowed atheists. The world applauds his
powerful intellect and admires his political and philosophical
sagacity. But God takes the measure of Karl Marx in one
word: Fool!

I think, also, of Frederick Nietzsche to whom Nazi
Germany was so deeply indebted. It was he who wrote:

> What distinguishes us is not that we do not
> rediscover any God either in nature or behind nature
> but that we recognize what was worshiped as God
> not as divine — but as pitiable, as absurd, as injur-
> ious — not only an error but a crime against life. We
> deny God as God.

It was he who also wrote:

> I call Christianity the one great curse, the one
> great depravity. — I call it the immortal blemish of
> mankind.

It was he who insisted that morality is nonsense, that might is right, and that the superman must ruthlessly smash his way to power, stopping at nothing in order to achieve his goal.

Even scholars who hate Naziism admit their intellectual indebtedness to Frederick Nietzsche. They praise his profundity and his wisdom, much as they may dislike the way Adolf Hitler utilized the doctrines of their master. God, on the other hand, takes the measure of Frederick Nietzsche in one word: Fool!

I think, yet again, of John Dewey, professor at Columbia University, whose educational theories influenced American schools to an incalculable degree. It was he who asserted that there is no absolute right and wrong, and there is no destiny for human beings beyond this present life any more than for a grasshopper or a tadpole. Thus he wrote:

> Faith in the divine author and authority in which Western civilization confided, inherited ideas of the soul and its destiny, of fixed revelation, of completely stable institutions — have been made impossible for the cultivated mind of the Western world.

He also wrote that there must be

> A surrender of that supernaturalism and fixed dogma and rigid institutionalism with which Christianity has been historically associated.

In a word, according to Professor Dewey, atheism is the only creed an intelligent man can now embrace. The world looked upon John Dewey as probably the most distinguished intellect in the United States. He was honored and revered to the point of fulsomeness. God, on the other hand, took the measure of John Dewey in one word: Fool!

The whole matter comes down to this: Is everything in the universe the product of chance, or is everything in the universe the production of an Almighty Creator? Creation or chance, those are the alternatives, and faced by those alternatives, common sense cries out, "God!"

The Scottish philosopher, Beattie, waited until his son was five years old before attempting to talk with him concerning God. Then, in order to pave the way for a conversation on this august subject, he secretly planted garden cress in such a way that on growing up it would spell out the three initials of the child's name. Even the five-year-old boy had sense enough to see that someone had planned that planting, and he was led to see God as his Creator. Then what about the universe and ourselves? Will chance explain us or must we acknowledge a Creator? Faced with that choice common sense cries out, "God!" Only a fool cries out "Chance!" As Gene Farrell exclaims in his poem, *Incredulity*:

> Beyond the awe-inspiring range
>   Of telescopic eyes,
> Great constellations wheel and spin
>   Through regimented skies.
>
> While here a pin-point miracle
>   Of microscopic clay,
> Alone in all the universe
>   Refuses to obey!
>
> Refuses to obey the One
>   Who said, "Let there be light!"

And instantly ten million stars
  Spake majesty and might!

Refuses to accept the One
  Who said, "Come unto Me,
And I will give you peace and joy
  Through all eternity!"

Almighty God and Saviour, too,
  Omnipotence and grace
Give chance to turn from chaos
  God's order to embrace.

Yet men prefer to disobey,
  Reject the gospel story,
Refuse to take eternal life,
  Abundant grace, and glory.

Paul was wholly justified in pronouncing upon the godless sages of this world the stinging sentence, "Professing themselves to be wise, they became fools."

My friends, may I in all kindness address a word of advice to each one of you personally? Do not be a fool! There is a God who made you and who will finally judge you. In fathomless love He gave His only-begotten Son, the Lord Jesus Christ, to die as our substitute so that by faith in that all-sufficient atonement you and I, meriting eternal death, might nonetheless have everlasting life. You may deny God, ignore Him, blaspheme Him, and completely forget Him. But some day you must and will face Him. I urge you, then, as Amos exhorted the ancient Israelites, "Prepare to meet thy God." And do it *now!*

The Wisdom of the World
(II)

IN HIS LETTER TO THE ROMANS, the apostle
Paul writes stingingly concerning the stupidity of
human wisdom. Listen to his castigation of man's reason
when it is not rooted and grounded in God:

> For the invisible things of him from the creation
> of the world are clearly seen, being understood by the
> things that are made, even his eternal power and God-
> head; so that they are without excuse: because that,
> when they knew God, they glorified him not as God,
> neither were thankful; but became vain in their imag-
> inations, and their foolish heart was darkened. Pro-
> fessing themselves to be wise, they became fools, and
> changed the glory of the uncorruptible God into an
> image made like to corruptible man and to birds,
> and fourfooted beasts, and creeping things.
>
> *Romans 1:20-23*

Yet how amazing it is that, when their minds are perverted by sinful pride, human beings will even stoop to the
senseless practice of idolatry. As Paul says, they change "the
glory of the uncorruptible God into an image made like

to corruptible man, and to birds, and fourfooted beasts, and creeping things."

Because he is incurably religious, man must worship something; and so, if he no longer worships his Creator, he makes idols before which he bows in adoration. India's Mahatma Gandhi was a powerful personality and undoubtedly possessed a brilliant mind. As a matter of fact, his admirers, who are legion, looked upon him as a twentieth-century saint whose every word was freighted down with the wisdom of the ages. He was educated in England and was graduated from one of its leading universities. He was a lawyer whose talents were internationally respected. Yet Gandhi once voyaged from Great Britain to India, spending his time squatting on deck, clad only in a loin cloth — making idols out of mud! He was thoroughly acquainted with the teachings of the gospel and repeatedly referred to the New Testament; but he turned his back upon the true and living God as revealed in Jesus Christ, and surrendered to Oriental superstitions. Professing himself to be wise, he indulged in the folly of idolatry. For all absurdities, the worship of a self-made image is by long odds the most stupid. Isaiah ironically exposes the folly of this in these famous words,

> They that fashion a graven image are all of them vanity; and the things that they delight in shall not profit; and their own witnesses see not, nor know: that they may be put to shame. Who hath fashioned a god, or molten an image that is profitable for nothing? Behold, all his fellows shall be put to shame; and the workmen, they are of men: let them all be gathered together, let them stand up; they shall fear, they shall be put to shame together. The

smith maketh an axe, and worketh in the coals, and
fashioneth it with hammers, and worketh it with his
strong arm: yea, he is hungry, and his strength faileth;
he drinketh no water, and is faint. The carpenter
stretcheth out a line; he marketh it out with a pencil;
he shapeth it with planes, and he marketh it out with
the compasses, and shapeth it after the figure of man,
according to the beauty of a man, to dwell in a house.
He heweth him down cedars, and taketh the holm-
tree and the oak, and strengtheneth for himself one
among the trees of the forest: he planteth a fir tree,
and the rain doth nourish it. Then shall it be for a
man to burn; and he taketh thereof, and warmeth
himself; yea, he kindleth it, and baketh bread: yea,
he maketh a god, and worshipeth it; he maketh it a
graven image, and falleth down thereto. He burneth
part thereof in the fire; with part thereof he eateth
flesh; he roasteth roast, and is satisfied; yea, he warmeth himself, and saith, Aha, I am warm, I have seen
the fire. And the residue thereof he maketh a god,
even his graven image; he falleth down unto it and
worshipeth, and prayeth unto it, and saith, Deliver
me; for thou art my god.

Isaiah 44:9-17

In the Union of Soviet Socialist Republics, as in our
own country, thousands of sophisticated citizens no longer
profess faith in God. They are too wise for that. But do
you know that while religion has declined, there has been
a corresponding and surprising growth in the crudest kind
of superstition? Too wise to believe in God, many of
Russia's enlightened atheists nevertheless put their trust
in the power of a rabbit's foot, or in the clairvoyance of an
astrologer. Listen to this statement from an official newspaper:

In schools just those children who are absolutely outside of any church influence prove to be the most inclined to the crudest superstitions. They do not believe in God, but they do believe in charms and amulets; they attribute no force to prayer, but a mystical connotation to meeting a funeral procession or dropping a book from a desk. They make magic knots and whisper magic formulae in order to prevent being asked the lesson.

And Dr. W. S. Timasheff, an authority on Russia, says:

Superstition is widespread among miners, sailors, drivers, fliers, and the like who boast of being atheists.

Here in the United States conditions are no different. I know of men who mock at God but who will not undertake a new venture on Friday, the thirteenth. I know of men who mock at God but run away from a black cat. I know of men who mock at God but make a long detour to avoid walking under a ladder. I know of men who mock at God but who are afraid of cemeteries. As Ray Tucker, one of Washington's best-known columnists, recently wrote in a syndicated article:

The most popular and profitable business in the capital today are those carried on by fortunetellers, palmists, astrologists, tealeaf diviners, and psychiatrists. Washington has gone "nuts" about foreseeing its personal and collective future.

Diplomats from foreign principalities first introduced the idea. They never threw a party without hiring a voodoo artist and esconcing her in an upstairs room where she psychoanalyzed the guests. Her fee was around twenty dollars, plus a bottle of good wine.

The fad has spread since Washington became the center of domestic and overseas leaders. They consult these stargazers regularly. Some of our topnotch officials frame their policies in accordance with the soothsayings of these oracles.

Consider that in turning away from the knowledge of the true and living God, men become fools because they do not know how to live decently or sanely. Centuries ago the prophet Jeremiah made a devastating comment regarding the nation Israel, which may be applied to the world at large:

> For my people is foolish, they have not known me; they are sottish children, and they have none understanding: they are wise to do evil, but to do good they have no knowledge.
>
> *Jeremiah 4:22*

Once men turn away from God, they lose the knowledge of how to do good, and they are wise only when it comes to doing evil. If you have any doubt about that, look out upon the world today where humanity with its perverted intelligence is engaged in self-destruction. When it comes to war, the nations function superbly, organizing their resources, mobilizing their armies, and inventing new instruments of destruction, astounding in their ingenuity. But when it comes to peace, the nations are baffled. They do not know how to cope with the problems of overproduction, unemployment, and depression. As Bishop Fulton J. Sheen has said:

> Never before has man had so much power, and never before has that power been so amassed for the destruction of human life. Never before has there been so much education and never before so little

coming to a knowledge of the truth. Never before
has there been so much wealth and never before so
much poverty. Never before did we have so much
food and never before so many hungry men. . . .
Man is surrounded by luxuries and conveniences of
which previous generations never dreamed, yet he
was never so frustrated, never so miserable, never
so uncertain of the future.

No wonder the famous French author, Lavredan, who
had long professed to be an atheist, when confronted by
the horrors of World War I during which he witnessed the
insane destruction in his own country, made this gripping
confession:

I laughed at faith and thought myself wise. Finally this laughter became hollow and vain for I saw
France bleeding and mourning. What would become
of France if her children did not believe, if her
women did not pray? Oh, a people whose fields are
covered with the dead! How difficult it is to remain
an atheist on this national cemetery! I cannot! I
cannot! I have deceived myself and you who have
read my book. It was a delusion, a giddiness, an
evil dream. I see death and call for life. Hands
equipped with weapons make death; folded hands
bring life. France, turn back to faith! To forsake
God means to be lost!

Surely Solomon knew whereof he spoke:

The fear of the Lord is the beginning of wisdom.
                                        Proverbs 9:10

This godless world of ours needs to have that thundered
into its ears continually. *The fear of the Lord is the begin-*

ning of wisdom. A man may know all the facts concerning history, philosophy, science, psychology, and literature. He may be a perambulating encyclopedia. But unless
he knows God, he is simply a learned ignoramous, a fool
puffed up in his own conceit. On the other hand, a man
may know nothing about history, philosophy, science,
psychology and literature; he may not know the alphabet
or the multiplication table; nor even how to write his own
name. Yet if he knows God, he is wiser than all of the
world's godless philosophers.

How, then, can a man know God? Not simply know
that He exists or know about Him, but really know God
in loving, intimate fellowship? Here is what Paul says:

> For after that in the wisdom of God the world
> by wisdom knew not God, it pleased God by the
> foolishness of preaching to save them that believe.
> For the Jews require a sign, and the Greeks seek
> after wisdom: but we preach Christ crucified, unto
> the Jews a stumblingblock, and unto the Greeks
> foolishness; but unto them which are called, both Jews
> and Greeks, Christ the power of God, and the wisdom
> of God.
>
> *1 Corinthians 1:21-24*

So, while Christianity is not at all irrational, we must
insist that man does not reason his way into fellowship
with God. A man comes to know God personally, inti-
mately, and redemptively only through the exercise of a
childlike trust. For, as Paul explains it, through the foolishness of the cross God has been pleased to save them that
believe. And when a man through faith in the all-pardon-
ing sacrifice of Calvary comes to know God, he is truly
wise because he possesses Christ in whom "are hid all the

treasures of wisdom and knowledge." Thus when by faith a man possesses Christ he likewise possesses, you see, the very wisdom of God; then, no matter what the foolish wisdom of the world may say, he knows that there is a God, and all the arguments of all the atheists cannot shake his serene assurance of God's reality. Once by faith a man possesses Jesus Christ, in whom are hidden all the treasures of wisdom and knowledge, then no matter what the foolish wisdom of the world may say, he knows that God is holy and hates sin. No matter what the foolish wisdom of the world may say, the saved person knows that God is merciful and loves sinners. He knows that God is infinitely gracious and that in His grace He gave His only begotten Son that whosoever believeth in Him should not perish, but have everlasting life. He knows that God is compassionate and that in His compassion he has provided perfect salvation through simple trust in the sacrifice of Calvary. He knows that God is all-forgiving and that in His forgiveness He has prepared a blessed eternity for all who will accept salvation in childlike fashion which is foolishness in the eyes of the world.

Mr. C. J. Pietsch, a Federal Housing Commissioner in Honolulu, distributed thousands upon thousands of copies of the New Testament among American sailors who were stationed in that city. On the day after Pearl Harbor was attacked, he received a request to visit one of the battleships. Arriving and going below, he found about four hundred men waiting for him, sitting on their bunks in rows five high. One of them spoke up as he entered:

> Mr. Pietsch, we sent for you because many of us have been heartsick, homesick, and seasick; and after what happened last night, we were all con-

cerned. Our country has provided for us, giving us food, clothing, a place to sleep; but no one has told us how to die. We would like you tell us. Many of us may never come back.

Ah, yes, when it comes to death, the insufficiency of this world's wisdom is starkly revealed, and then it is that every man longs for a faith which will enable him to say:

Yea, though I walk through the valley of the shadow of death, I will fear no evil: for thou art with me; thy rod and thy staff they comfort me.

Psalm 23:4

Do not wait until that dark hour overtakes you. Turn in faith to Jesus Christ now, accept Him as your Saviour, and by His grace live victoriously and die triumphantly.